The Poetry Chest

For Chris

The Poetry Chest

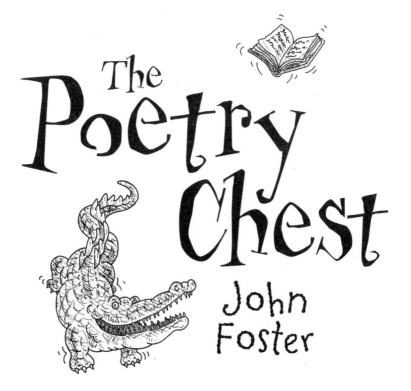

John Foster

OXFORD
UNIVERSITY PRESS

OXFORD

UNIVERSITY PRESS

Great Clarendon Street, Oxford OX2 6DP

Oxford University Press is a department of the University of Oxford.
It furthers the University's objective of excellence in research, scholarship,
and education by publishing worldwide in

Oxford   New York

Auckland   Cape Town   Dar es Salaam   Hong Kong   Karachi
Kuala Lumpur   Madrid   Melbourne   Mexico City   Nairobi
New Delhi   Shanghai   Taipei   Toronto

With offices in

Argentina   Austria   Brazil   Chile   Czech Republic   France   Greece
Guatemala   Hungary   Italy   Japan   Poland   Portugal   Singapore
South Korea   Switzerland   Thailand   Turkey   Ukraine   Vietnam

Oxford is a registered trade mark of Oxford University Press
in the UK and in certain other countries

British Library Cataloguing in Publication Data

Data available

ISBN: 978-0-19-276341-9

11

Printed in Great Britain

Paper used in the production of this book is a natural,
recyclable product made from wood grown in sustainable forests.
The manufacturing process conforms to the environmental
regulations of the country of origin.

Contents

Football Poems 83

Poems About Our World

Weather Poems

Seasons Poems   147

Animal Poems   159

Dinosaur and Dragon Poems   175

Wizard, Ghost, and Vampire Poems   187

SECTION 2
– DIFFERENT TYPES OF POEMS

199

Nonsense Poems

201

Wordplay Poems

213

Riddles and Puzzle Poems   233

Punctuation and Spelling Poems 241

Poetry Patterns 251

■ TANKA

■ TONGUE-TWISTERS

■ STORY POEMS

Introduction

T*he Poetry Chest* is a collection of poems for you
to read on your own or to share with your
classmates at school, or at home with your family
and friends. All of them are poems that I have written
myself and many of them are ones that I've read and
performed during my visits to schools and libraries and
at literary festivals throughout Britain.

To help you find your way into *The Poetry Chest* we've
divided the book into two parts. In the first part, you'll
find poems on all kinds of different themes, from pets
to parents, from wizards to the weather and from
dinosaurs to football. There are plenty of humorous
poems, but there are serious poems too, on subjects
such as bullying, war and the environment.

In the second half of the book, you'll find a range of
different types of poems. For example, there are nonsense
poems and story poems, poems that use wordplay,
poems presented as riddles or puzzles, and poems in a
variety of patterns, such as limericks and tongue-twisters.

At the back of the book, there is an index of poem
types, which will help you if you're looking for a
particular type of poem. There's also a glossary of poetry
terms, explaining poetic forms, such as acrostics,
epitaphs and haiku, as well as the meaning of words
used to describe how language is used in poetry, such
as alliteration, metaphor and simile.

The collection contains a number of poems that can be used as a framework for writing your own poems. If you want to have a try at writing some poems of your own, you'll find some ideas that may help you to get started in the section 'Writing poems of your own' at the back of the book.

One of the questions I'm frequently asked is 'Where do you get your ideas from?' Getting an idea for a poem isn't always easy. They come in three different ways. Firstly, they come from your own experience. In the Family poems section, there's a poem called 'The Vase'. It's about sitting waiting for Mum to come back and wondering how to tell her that you've broken a vase that was one of her treasured possessions, because it was given to her as a wedding present. I once had that experience!

Secondly, your ideas come from your observations – things that you hear or see. One day I was in a school and I saw a picture of the tropical rainforest that was being cut down in order to build a new highway. It set me thinking about the destruction of the rainforest and that led to my poem 'Where Is the Forest?' Then there are the poems about bullying. They are all based on my observations of pupils who were being bullied during the time I was a teacher.

Thirdly, your ideas come from your imagination. For example, in my poem 'Interview with a Dragon', I just imagined what questions an interviewer might ask and the replies that a dragon might give.

Another question I'm frequently asked is: Why do you write poetry? One of the main reasons is because

I like words. I like playing with words, their sounds and their meanings, from making up batty booklists to writing nonsense poems about what's going on 'In the Land of the Flibbertigibbets'.

Whatever your reason for picking up this book, whether you are an aspiring poet yourself, or you just like reading poems, because you find them entertaining and thought-provoking, I hope you enjoy reading these poems as much as I have enjoyed writing them.

JOHN FOSTER
May 2007

School Poems

War Poems

Bullying Poems

Seasons Poems

Poems About Our World

SECTION 1
– THEMES

Family Poems

My Mum Says

My mum says:

If you don't pick up your pyjamas
and fold them under your pillow,
I'll throw them out of the window
for the binmen to pick up.

If you don't go upstairs
and get washed immediately,
I'll take you out into the garden
and turn the hosepipe on you.

If you don't hurry up
and get dressed at once,
I'll take you to school
in your knickers.

If you're not out of this door
in ten seconds' time,
I'll kiss you goodbye outside school.

My mum says:

You think I'm joking, don't you.

You Little Monkey!

My mum said
I was behaving
like a little monkey.

So I climbed
onto the sofa
and started swinging
on the door.

When she told me to stop,
I made chattering noises
and pretended to
scratch my armpits.

I refused
to talk properly
until tea-time,
when all I got
was a plate of nuts
and a banana!

So I decided
to stop
monkeying about.

Chinese, Please!

Chinese, please!
Chinese, please!
We want Chinese for our teas.
Oodles of noodles,
Chicken and rice,
We think Chinese meals are nice!

Chinese, please!
Chinese, please!
We want Chinese for our teas.
Beef chop suey,
Chicken chow mein,
Please can we have Chinese again!

Making Waves

This evening,
Instead of washing my hair
I slid up and down the bath
To see how big a wave
I could make.

Water splashed
Over the side of the bath
And started dripping
Through the kitchen ceiling.

That's why I'm up here
Lying in the dark, thinking,
While everyone else
Is downstairs
Watching telly.

Bedtime Story

Last night,
My mum blew up,
She caught me still reading at midnight.
'That's it, my girl,' she stormed.
'If I ever catch you doing that again,
You're for it.'

This morning,
She charged into my room
And unscrewed the light bulbs.
'From now on,' she said,
'You can get dressed and undressed in the dark.
That'll teach you
To go on reading till all hours.'

This afternoon,
I emptied my piggy bank
And went down town
To buy myself a torch.

It's now a quarter to one.
It's stuffy down here under the bedclothes
And I'm feeling drowsy.
But there's only twenty pages to go
And I must find out what happens.

This Morning My Dad Shouted

This morning my Dad shouted.
This morning my Dad swore.
There was water through the ceiling.
There was water on the floor.
There was water on the carpets.
There was water down the stairs.
The kitchen stools were floating,
So were the dining chairs.

This morning I've been crying,
Dad made me so upset.
He shouted and he swore at me
Just 'cause things got so wet.
I only turned the tap on
To get myself a drink.
The trouble is I didn't see
The plug was in the sink.

Present Smugglers

This morning,
While Mum was having a lie-in,
Because it's Saturday,
My sister and I
Emptied our money-boxes
And went down town
To buy the scarf
We know she'll like.

When we got home,
My sister went in first
And kept her talking,
While I smuggled the scarf upstairs
And hid it in the shoe-box
Under my bed.

This afternoon,
We'll go down to the flower shop with Dad
And we'll smuggle a plant
Into the shed.

Tonight,
We'll write the cards
We smuggled in
Earlier in the week
And wrap up the scarf.

Then, in the morning,
We'll give ourselves up,
Hand over the smuggled goods
And watch Mum's face
As she opens her presents
On Mother's Day.

The Vase

We've picked up all the pieces.
We've brushed and swept the floor.
We're waiting, listening for the click
Of Mum's key in the door.

We're wondering how to tell her.
We're wondering how to say
We broke the vase her Grandma gave her
On her wedding day.

My Baby Brother's Secrets

When my baby brother
wants to tell me a secret,
he comes right up close.
But instead of putting his lips
against my ear,
he presses his ear
tightly against my ear.
Then, he whispers so softly
that I can't hear
a word he's saying.

My baby brother's secrets
are safe with me.

Talking to the Wall

My sister sits in her own world
With her Walkman blaring away
And when we try to talk to her
She doesn't hear a word we say.

But when she wants to talk to us
She pulls her earphones out
And if we do not answer her
She stamps her foot and shouts.

Sarah, My Sister, Has Asthma

Sarah, my sister, has asthma.
Sometimes, I wake up in the night
And hear her wheezing
In the bunk below.

I remember the time
I woke to hear her gasping for breath
And Mum had to call an ambulance.
They took her to the hospital
And kept her in for tests.

'She's allergic,' the doctor said.
'I expect she'll grow out of it.
Most children do.'

Now she carries an inhaler
Everywhere she goes.

She gets annoyed when people
Try to stop her doing things.
She's always telling Grandma
To stop fussing.

'I'm not different,' she says.
'It's only asthma.
Lots of people have it.'

On Sports Day
Sarah came first in the high jump.
'You see, I'm not different,' she said.

Sarah, my sister, has asthma.
Sometimes, I wake up in the night
And hear her wheezing
In the bunk below.

Just Because You're My Sister

Just because you're my sister,
Why should I do what you do?
Just because you're my sister,
Why should I behave like you?

Everyone goes on and on
About how well you've done,
About the exams you've passed
And all the trophies you've won.

Why can't they leave me alone?
Why can't everyone see
I don't want to be a copy of you.
I just want to be valued as me.

In My Dream

In my dream,
My older brother is racing along a sandy beach,
Whooping and laughing.

I am trying to keep up with him,
But he is drawing further and further away.

I call for him to wait,
But the wind whisks away my words.

When I tell my mother,
She hugs me.

'Don't worry,' she says.
'All in good time, your turn will come.'

There Are Four Chairs Round the Table

There are four chairs round the table,
Where we sit down for our tea.
But now we only set places
For Mum, for Terry and me.

We don't chatter any more
About what we did in the day.
Terry and I eat quickly,
Then we both go out to play.

Mum doesn't smile like she used to.
Often, she just sits and sighs.
Sometimes, I know from the smudges,
That while we are out she cries.

Every Other Sunday

Every other Sunday
I stand and wait
For Dad to pick me up
Down by the front gate.

If the weather is fine,
We visit the park or zoo.
When it rains, we sit in a café
Wondering what to do.

He asks me about school
And what I've done this week.
But everything's different now
And we find it hard to speak.

Every other Sunday,
Dead on half-past four
Dad drops me outside the house
And waits till I've gone in the door.

Somehow It's Not the Same

On Sundays when we go to the park
We play a football game.
My step-dad always plays with me,
But somehow it's not the same.

Sometimes we'll go down the pond
To sail the models he's made.
But somehow it's not the same
As the games my dad and I played.

He takes me for burger and chips
And pays for my rides at the fair.
But somehow it's not the same
As it was when my dad took me there.

Parents!

Parents!
They're so embarrassing.

When my dad sneezes,
He makes such a racket
It's as if a minor explosion
Has been detonated
Inside his nose.
Then he whips out
His handkerchief with a flourish
And trumpets loudly,
Shattering the silence
With his coughing, spluttering and wheezing.

As for my mum,
Her stomach gurgles and rumbles
Like a broken cistern
That never stops filling.
It saves the loudest churnings
For that moment's silence
In the middle of a concert
Or the most dramatic moment
At the climax of a play,
So people turn and frown
Or pretend not to notice,

Though they couldn't help but have heard,
And I go bright red,
Wishing the ground would open up
And swallow me,
Or that I was cool and confident enough
To look disdainful,
As if to say:
She's not my mum, you know,
Don't blame me!

Parents!
They're so embarrassing.

Why Is It?

Why is it
That when we go to the park
to fly my kite
the string always gets tangled
in the trees
and the kite gets torn
while other kids' kites
go soaring and swooping?

Why is it
that when we play cricket
on the beach
my dad always drops catches
and is out first ball,
while other kids' dads
hit the ball
over the breakwater
into the sea?

Why is it
that when my mum asks my dad
to put up a picture
on the wall,
he drills a hole
that's far too big
and gets plaster everywhere?

But when my dad
tells my brother and me stories
in the dark,
why is it
I can almost see
the creatures
and feel their hot breath?

My Cousins

When my three cousins come to stay,
  the house bubbles with their chatter,
    rings with their laughter
      and squawks with their squabbling.

When my three cousins go home,
  the house regains its composure
    and, with a subdued sigh,
      relaxes into its routine rhythm.

Grandma Is a Warm Scarf

Grandma is navy blue.
She is a comfy cushion.
Grandma is a soft whisper.
She is a path through a winter wood.
Grandma is a warm scarf.
She is a cup of tea by the fire.
Grandma is a sleeping cat.
She is autumn sunshine.

Waking at Gran's

Sometimes,
When I stay at Gran's,
I wake up in the morning
And can't remember
Where I am.

I feel a moment's fear
That overnight
Someone has changed
The colour of the curtains
Re-papered the walls
And moved the door of the bedroom.

Then I hear Gran
Moving about downstairs
Chattering to the budgie,
As she makes my breakfast.

At once,
The world snaps into focus:
I know where I am
And that last night
I slept in the bedroom at Gran's
Where Mum used to sleep
When she was little
And my fear
Disappears.

Grandma's Doll

Grandma's doll has a blue cotton dress
And a white lace bonnet.

Her body is stuffed with straw
And feels stiff and hard.

Her head is made of china
And there are tiny cracks
All over her face.

'They look like wrinkles,'
I said.

'That's because she's old,'
Laughed Grandma.
'Like me.'

How Old Are You Grandad?

'How old are you Grandad?'
my little sister asked.
Grandad grinned.
'As old as my tongue,' he said.
'And nearly as old as my teeth.'
'What about your hair?' she asked.
Grandad laughed
and stroked his bald head.
'That's a different matter,' he said.

Borrowed Time

Great-Gran is ninety-six.
'I'm living on borrowed time,'
she said.

'Who did you borrow it from?'
asked my little sister.

'Never you mind,' said Gran.

'I hope you said thank you,'
said my sister.

Great-Gran laughed.
'I do,' she said.
'Every single day.'

Great-Grandad's Memories

Great-Grandad forgets
The time of the day,
Where was going,
What he wanted to say.

Great-Grandad forgets
The day of the week.
He cannot recall
What we say when we speak.

Great-Grandad forgets
What he wants to do.
Sometimes when he sees me
He thinks that I'm you.

But Great-Grandad remembers
The relief and delight
The day the war ended
And they partied all night.

Great-Grandad remembers
How as a young man
He first met the girl
Who is now our great-gran.

Great-Grandad remembers
How things used to be
And I smile as he tells
His memories to me.

Great-Gran Just Sits

Great-Gran just sits
All day long there,
Beside the fire,
Propped in her chair.

Sometimes she mumbles
Or gives a shout,
But we can't tell
What it's about.

Great-Gran just sits
All day long there.
Her face is blank,
An empty stare.

When anyone speaks,
What does she hear?
When Great-Gran starts,
What does she fear?

How can we tell?
For we can't find
A key which can
Unlock her mind.

Great-Gran just sits,
Almost alone,
In some dream world
All of her own.

But when Mum bends
Tucking her rug
Perhaps she senses
That loving hug.

My Gramp

My Gramp has got a medal.
On the front there is a runner.
On the back it says:
Senior Boys 100 Yards
First William Green.
I asked him about it,
but before he could reply
Gran said, 'Don't listen to his tales.
The only running he did was after the girls.'
Gramp gave a chuckle
and went out the back
to get the tea.
As he shuffled down the passage
with his back bent,
I tried to imagine him,
legs flying, chest out,
breasting the tape.
But I couldn't.

Farewell Visit

The day before the bulldozers moved in,
Great-Grandpa took me across town by bus
To see the terraced house
Where he lived as a boy.

He pointed out where the standpipe was
And told me about the copper in the yard,
How he and his brothers shared a tin bath
Once a week.

He showed me where the privy stood
And the shed where they kept the coal
For the range on which his mother cooked
For a family of eight.

The house itself was empty,
Stripped bare, its windows boarded.
But in the yard
We found the remains of a mangle.

As we walked back to the bus-stop,
Great-Grandpa peopled the street with his memories.

Feelings
Poems

I'm In a Mood Today

I'm in a mood today.
I don't want to come out and play.
I don't care that it's sunny,
I'm feeling funny.
I'm in a mood today.

I'm in a mood today.
I don't care what Mum and Dad say.
I don't care if they shout
I'm *not* going out.
I'm in a mood today.

I'm in a mood today.
Why can't you just go away?
I want to be on my own.
Just leave me alone.
I'm in a mood today.

Moods

Some days
A dark cloud
Fills my mind.
Everything's dull
As if someone
Has drawn a blind
Blotting out the sunlight.

Other days
A stream of light
Fills my mind.
Everything's bright
As if someone
Has thrown open the shutters
Letting the sunlight pour in.

Anger

Anger
Is a red bull
Charging through the mind's fields,
Inciting actions you may soon
Regret.

Why Did You Pull Her Hair?

I told my friend a secret.
She promised not to tell.
My friend told her friend.
She told her friend as well.

Now, everyone knows my secret.
I think that it's unfair.
I told my friend I trusted her.
That's why I pulled her hair.

The Worries

At night-time, as I lie in bed,
The Worries swirl around my head:

What if I'm late for school?
What if I blush and feel a fool?

What if I fail the test?
What if I did not try my best?

What if they call me names?
What if I can't join in their games?

What if my report's bad?
What if my Dad gets very mad?

What if aliens kidnap me?
What if I shrink to the size of a pea?

What if I'm attacked by a shark?
What if I start to glow in the dark?

What if I grow a beard overnight?
What if a vampire gives me a bite?

What if I'm woken by a scream?
What if it's *real* and not a dream?

At night-time, as I lie in bed,
The Worries swirl around my head.

The Cellar

The cellar is gloomy.
The cellar is deep.
Down in the cellar
There are things that creep.

Down in the cellar
There is no light.
Down in the cellar
It's as dark as night.

Down in the cellar
It's icy cold.
The walls are damp
And covered in mould.

Down in the cellar
Who knows what's there,
Down at the foot
Of the creaking stair.

So please don't ask me,
Please don't dare,
Please don't dare me
To go down there.

Holidays

Happy-go-lucky days.
Off out and about days.
Lazy lie-in-bed days.
In front of TV days.
Do as you please days.
Away to the sea days.
You can choose what to do days.
School's over! We're free days!

The Shell

On the shelf in my bedroom stands a shell.
If I hold it close, I can smell
The salty sea.
I can hear the slap
Of the waves as they lap
The sandy shore.
I can feel once more
The tickling tide
As it gently flows between my toes.

I Stood All Alone in the Playground

I stood all alone in the playground
At breaktime today.
I didn't feel like playing the games
The others wanted to play.

I stood all alone in the playground,
Trying not to cry,
Thinking of Nan and wondering why
Old people have to die.

My Little Sister

My little sister used to get on my nerves.

She'd borrow things without asking,
then put them back in the wrong place.

When my friends came round,
she'd pester them
until they'd let her play with them.

If there was something I wanted to watch,
she'd refuse to change channels
unless I bribed her.

When she woke up in the middle of the night,
she'd crawl in beside me
and wake me up with her wriggling.

My little sister used to get on my nerves.
But the bedroom seems so empty without her
And I miss her terribly.

Hospital Visit

Beneath the thinning hair,
A puzzled stare,
A searching frown
As Grandpa looks me up and down.

Catching at last a clue
Within my face,
My name slots into place:
'Ah, Jack, it's you.'

A brief light in his eyes
As Grandpa talks,
Recalling fishing trips and walks
Along the clifftop.

Grandpa sighs,
Lies back against the pillow.
Face pale as the sheets,
He drifts asleep.

A nurse appears.
'He tires fast, you know.'
Eyes filling up with tears,
I turn and go.

There's a New Wooden Seat

There's a new wooden seat
Down by the church gate
Where I sometime sit
If the bus is late.

And I read the words
Of the bright brass plaque:
In Loving Memory
Of Stanley Black.

And I think of the man
With the silvery hair,
Who used to enjoy
The view from there.

And I smile recalling
The pleasure I had
When I stood there
Beside Grandad.

Moving On

It's time to go.
I take one last look round.
The bare floorboards creak—
An eerie sound.

For the very last time
I close the door
Of the room that now
Isn't my room any more.

I pause on the landing.
Outside the horn blares.
Lost deep in my memories
I hurry downstairs.

I close the front door
And the house that was home
Slips into the past
Where only ghosts roam.

How Strange

How strange to think that someone else
Lived in this house before,
That other people climbed these stairs
And stood on my bedroom floor.

Who was the child who once slept here?
Was it a girl or boy?
What were the dreams that they dreamed?
What was their favourite toy?

How strange to think that someone else
Will live here when I've gone.
Will no one feel my presence here
When I'm the one who's moved on?

School
Poems

Our Teacher's Gone Bananas

Our teacher, Mr Mann,
Thinks he's an orang-utan.

When we do P.E.,
He climbs up the wall bars
And swings on the ropes.

When we do Geography,
He talks about jungles
And gets a faraway look in his eyes.

When he takes assembly,
He hires a costume from Parties R Us
And talks about animal rights.

Our teacher has gone bananas.
There's nothing we can do.
Our teacher shouldn't be in a school,
He should be in a zoo.

Children's Prayer

Let the teachers of our class
Set us tests that we all pass.
Let them never ever care
About what uniform we wear.
Let them always clearly state
It's OK if your homework's late.
Let them say it doesn't matter
When we want to talk and chatter.

Let our teachers shrug and grin
When we make an awful din.
Let them tell us every day
There are no lessons. Go and play.
Let them tell our mum and dad
We're always good and never bad.
Let them write in their report
We are the best class they have taught!

Teachers!
I Don't Understand Them

Teachers!
I don't understand them.

They say:
   When you hand in your work,
   Make sure it's neat and tidy.
Then they mess it up
By scribbling illegible comments
All over it in red ink.

They say:
   Don't interrupt when I'm talking.
   Put your hand up
   And wait until I've finished.
But if they've got something to say,
They clap their hands
And stop your discussions in mid-sentence.

They say:
   Always plan your writing.
   Take your time. Think it through
   And do a rough draft.
Then they sit you in an examination hall
And ask you to write an essay
On one of six topics –
None of which interests you –
In an hour and a quarter.

They say:
    All work and no play
    Makes Jill a dull girl.
    Make sure you allow yourself
    Time off from your studies
    To relax and enjoy yourself.
Then, when you don't hand
Your homework in on time,
Because you took their advice,
They keep you in at lunch-time.

Teachers!
I don't understand them.

Our Teacher's a Caterpillar

Our teacher's a caterpillar.
During the day she crawls
Between the leaves of our desks
Picking holes in our writing
And chewing over our attempts
To wrestle meaning from our number-work.
At home-time she scuttles to the staffroom
And pulls on her overcoat
Like a chrysalis.
Later, in the quiet of her bedroom,
She transforms herself
Into a butterfly
Which dances the night away.
On the stroke of midnight,
She turns back into a caterpillar,
Crawls home to bed and sleeps
Until the alarm-bell rings
Summoning her to another morning's school.

Watch It, Miss, Or Else!

Don't tell me off for shouting, miss,
Or I'll be forced to say
What I heard you call the referee
At the match on Saturday.

Don't give me extra homework, miss,
Don't you ever, ever dare
Or else I'll have to tell the class
About the wig you wear.

Don't keep me in at playtime, miss,
'Cause I couldn't do that sum
Or else I'll have to tell the head
That you were chewing gum.

Don't make me do my spellings again
Or I will have, I fear,
To tell the inspector how you spelt
'Disapoint' and 'disapear'.

Don't ever pick on me again
Or else I'll have to tell
I saw you kissing Mr West
Down by the wishing-well!

Hello, Mr Visitor

Hello, Mr Visitor
Have you come to visit Miss?
Are you her boyfriend?
D'you want to give her a kiss?

Are you a parent
Who's come up to complain?
Or are you the plumber
Who's come to fix the drain?

Are you an inspector
Who's come to test our skill?
Is that why the headteacher
Is looking pale and ill?

Are you the dreaded ghost
Of the teacher who said:
'You'll be the death of me!'
And dropped down dead?

Hello, Mr Visitor
Who would you like to see?
Welcome to our school
Whoever you may be!

Inside Sir's Matchbox

Our teacher's pet
Lives in a nest of pencil-shavings
Inside a matchbox
Which he keeps
In the top drawer of his desk.
It's so tiny, he says,
You need a microscope to see it.
When we asked him what it ate,
He grinned and said,
'Nail clippings and strands of human hair –
Especially children's.'
Once, on Open Day,
He put it out on the display table,
But we weren't allowed to open the box,
Because it's allergic to light.

Our teacher says his pet's unique.
'Isn't it lonely?' we asked.
'Not with you lot around,' he said.

Once, there was an awful commotion
When it escaped
While he was opening the box
To check if it was all right.
But he managed to catch it
Before it got off his desk.

Since then, he hasn't taken it out much.
He says he thinks it's hibernating at present –
Or it could be pregnant.
If it is, he says,
There'll be enough babies
For us all to have one.

Size-Wise

Our teacher Mr Little's really tall.
He's twice the size of our helper Mrs Small.
'Were you big when you were little?'
Sandra asked him.
'I was Little when I was little,
but I've always been big!'
he said with a grin.
'Have you always been small?'
Sandra asked Mrs Small.
'No,' said Mrs Small.
'I was Short before I got married,
then I became Small.
But,' she added, 'I've always been little.'
'That's the long and the short of it,'
said Mr Little.
'I've always been big and Little,
but she used to be little and Short,
and now she's little and Small.'

Why Do Teachers Call Me Emma?

Why do teachers call me Emma?
Emma isn't my name.
Though Emma and I are both tall and dark,
We don't really look the same.

Why do teachers call me Emma?
Why doesn't it occur
I'm not giggly and silly like Emma?
I'm not at all like her.

Why do teachers call me Emma?
Surely they can see
Outside I'm a bit like Emma,
But inside I'm Susan. I'm ME!

The Test

I'm not looking forward to tomorrow,
For tomorrow we've got the Test.
Mum's told me to try not to worry
And just to do my best.

But I can't get to sleep for wondering
What the questions will be,
And what if my friends all pass and go
To a different school from me.

It's no good pretending I'll ever
Come out top of the class.
I only hope that I get enough marks
To be one of the few who pass.

The Bell

I am the bell.
I rule the school.

When I ring,
Classes snap to attention.
Anyone who ignores me
Risks a detention.

When I ring,
Latecomers start running.
Teachers put down their coffee cups
And sigh.
Playground games stop.
Children line up.

I am the bell.
I carve the day into chunks.
I summon everyone to assembly
And decide when it's time for dinner.

I'm in control.
Everyone listens to me.
With my shrill voice
I can empty the playground
And the staffroom.

In an emergency,
I can clear the whole school
In less than three minutes.

I am the bell.
I rule the school.

Locked Out!

(For Mrs H.)

Our teacher's trapped in the playground.
She was late coming in from play.
The security door's been locked now.
She'll have to stay out all day!

Our teacher's trapped in the playground.
That's why she's got a big grin.
She's turning cartwheels and skipping about
'Cause she doesn't want to come in.

The Rules That Rule the School

Only speak when you're spoken to.
Don't stand and grin like a fool.
Pay attention or risk a detention.
We're the rules that rule the school.

Hands must not be in pockets
When addressing a member of staff.
Though smiling is sometimes permitted,
You need written permission to laugh.

Boys must stand to attention
And salute when they pass the Head.
Girls are expected to curtsy
And lower their eyes instead.

Sit up straight. Do as you're told,
If you want to come top of the class.
Bribes must be paid in cash
If you want to be sure to pass.

Don't breathe too loud in lessons.
Don't sweat too much in games.
Remember that teachers are human.
Don't *ever* call them names.

Only speak when you're spoken to.
Don't stand and grin like a fool.
Pay attention or risk a detention.
We're the rules that rule the school.

Teacher

Tells us off.
Expects us to know the answers.
Always asking questions.
Crosses out our mistakes.
Hands out detentions.
Explodes if we chew gum.
Rapidly ageing.

Writing and Sums

When the teacher asks us to write,
The words dance in my head,
Weaving neat patterns,
Gliding into their places,
Before flowing down my pencil
In an orderly procession.
But…
When the teacher tells me to do sums,
The figures fly round my head,
Fluttering like birds
Trapped behind glass,
Before escaping down my pencil
In frightened confusion.

Scene-Switching

Standing outside the Head's office,
I wish that I could fast forward
Through the scene
In which she's going to tell me off
And decide what punishment to give me.

Or that I could rewind the tape
To before break,
Then replay the scene
In which Tracey and I quarrelled.

Only this time, I'd play it differently.

Not the Answer

Why is it
that when there's a fight
in the playground
everyone gathers round
and starts taking sides,
even though most of them
don't know who started it
or what it's about?

Why is it
that when there's a fight
in the playground
I join the others
and race to watch and cheer
even though I know
deep down inside
fighting's not the answer?

I Dreamed a Dolphin

Yesterday,
On the way to school,
I dreamed a dolphin
That cavorted happily all day,
Swimming and singing.

When I went through the school gates,
The nets ensnared me.
I spent the day
Wallowing in the shallows,
An ordinary fish.

The Schoolkids' Rap

Miss was at the blackboard writing with the chalk,
When suddenly she stopped in the middle of her talk.
She snapped her fingers – snap! snap! snap!
Pay attention children and I'll teach you how to rap.

She picked up a pencil, she started to tap.
All together children, now clap! clap! clap!
Just get the rhythm, just get the beat.
Drum it with your fingers, stamp it with your feet.

That's right, children, keep in time.
Now we've got the rhythm, all we need is the rhyme.
This school is cool, Miss Grace is ace.
Strut your stuff with a smile on your face.

Snap those fingers, tap those toes.
Do it like they do it in the TV shows.
Flap it! Slap it! Clap! Snap! Clap!
Let's all do the schoolkids' rap!

Football
Poems

The Night Before the Match

The night before the match
I lie awake in bed
With thoughts of what might happen
Whirling round my head.

What if there's an open goal
And somehow I fail to score?
What if I miss a penalty
And we lose instead of draw?

What if I miss a tackle
And give a goal away?
What if I get a red card?
What will people say?

What if I'm clean through
And I slip and tread on the ball?
What if I'm ill in the morning
And can't even play at all?

The night before the match
It's always the same.
Why can't I feel like Dad who says:
'Don't worry. It's only a game.'

Kicking In

I'm kicking my ball
against the wall
against the wall and back.

I'm practising how
to pass the ball
by kicking the ball
against the wall
against the wall and back.

I'm practising how
to launch an attack
by passing the ball
against the wall
and running to get it back.

I'm dribbling the ball
towards the wall
around the dustbin and back.

I'm beating defenders
one and all
as I dribble the ball
towards the wall
around the dustbin and back.

I imagine the goalie
coming out.
I hear the fans
all cheer and shout.
I shoot the ball
towards the wall.
He dives too late.
It's through the gate!
And I've scored! I've scored! I've scored!

The Night I Won the Cup

Last night I had a wonderful dream,
Dreamed I was the captain of the England football team.
Running on the pitch, feeling ever so proud,
Hearing the roar of the capacity crowd

Shouting, cheering,
Booing, jeering,
Oohing and aahing,
As the game got underway.

It was nearly full-time. There was still no score.
It looked like we'd have to settle for a draw.
From deep in defence we developed an attack.
I jinked and I swerved. I was past their full-back.

And the crowd started shouting:

Whack it! Smack it!
Give it all you've got!
Swerve it! Curve it!
Go on! Take a shot!

The goalie rushed out to do the best he could.
I kept my head down as a striker should.
Into the net, the football soared.
The crowd went mad. Everyone roared:

It's a goal! It's a goal!
He's scored! He's scored!
They were hand-clapping, back-slapping,
Yelling, jumping up.
He's done it! We've won it!
We've won the cup!

I raised my fist to punch the air
And suddenly my Dad was standing there
Saying, 'Wake up! Wake up! What's up, our kid?
You sound as if you'd won the cup.'
'Dad,' I said, 'I did!'

Saturdays

Every Saturday, it's the same –
Worrying about the game.
Will we win? Will we draw?
Will we lose? Who will score?

Some Saturdays I get the blues
That's because United lose.
Some Saturdays I get to grin
That's because United win.

Football Story

This is the foot.

This is the foot
That kicked the ball.

This is the foot
That kicked the ball
That scored the goal.

This is the foot
That kicked the ball
That scored the goal
That won the cup.

This is the foot
That kicked the ball
That scored the goal
That won the cup
The day that the final
Was played in our yard.

This is the ball.

This is the ball
That was kicked by the foot
That scored the goal
That won the cup
The day that the final
Was played in our yard.

This is the ball
That flew over the fence
When kicked by the foot
That scored the goal
That won the cup
The day that the final
Was played in our yard.

This is the ball
That flew over the fence
And smashed the window
Of next door's kitchen
When kicked by the foot
That scored the goal
That won the cup
The day that the final
Was played in our yard.

This is the boy.

This is the boy
Who ran away.

This is the boy
Who ran away
To hide in the shed
When he heard the crash
Made by the ball
That flew over the fence
And smashed the window
Of next door's kitchen
When kicked by the foot
That scored the goal
That won the cup
The day that the final
Was played in our yard.

This is the father.

This is the father
Who found the boy
Who ran away
To hide in the shed
When he heard the crash
Made by the ball
That flew over the fence
And smashed the window
Of next door's kitchen
When kicked by the foot
That scored the goal
That won the cup
The day that the final
Was played in our yard.

This is the father
Who dragged home the boy
Who ran away
To hide in the shed
When he heard the crash
Made by the ball
That flew over the fence
And smashed the window
Of next door's kitchen
When kicked by the foot
That scored the goal
That won the cup
The day that the final
Was played in our yard.

This is the hand.

This is the hand
Of the boy
Who ran away
To hide in the shed
When he heard the crash
Made by the ball
That flew over the fence
And smashed the window
Of next door's kitchen
When kicked by the foot
That scored the goal
That won the cup
The day that the final
Was played in our yard.

This is the hand
Of the boy
Who went round
To knock on the door
Of the neighbour's house
To say
'Please can I have my ball back.'

Please, Mr Black

Mr Black, Mr Black,
Please can we have our football back.
You can pass it through the window.
It'll fit through the crack.
Oh, don't be a spoilsport, Mr Black.
Please can we have our football back.

Pride Comes Before a Fall

'Pride comes before a fall,'
My dad used to say
Whenever my little brother
Started showing off.

Now dad sits on the sofa,
Looking sheepish,
With his leg propped on a stool
And his toes sticking out of the plaster.

Last week,
As he was prancing round the garden
Pretending he was David Beckham,
He trod on the ball.
He fell awkwardly
And broke his ankle.

'Don't expect any sympathy from me,'
Said my mum.
'You should know better at your age.'

'Pride comes before a fall,'
Says my brother
On his way out
To play football with his friends.

The World's Best

My dad's the world's best,
He's a football referee.
He referees internationals
From a seat on our settee.

An hour before the kick-off
He gets changed into his kit.
He then inspects the room
And tells us where to sit.

As we watch the pre-match build-up,
He waits beside the door,
Until the teams come out
Then he strides across the floor.

He stands to attention
While the national anthems play,
Then takes his seat on the settee
As the game gets underway.

His eagle eyes spot every foul
The opposition makes.
He's very quick to point out
The real ref's mistakes.

He won't stand for any nonsense.
On dissent he's very hard.
If we challenge his decisions,
He shows us a red card.

But sometimes he forgets
His self-appointed role
By letting out a mighty roar
When England score a goal.

Colour Blind

Football referees
Are peculiar fellows.
They think a red card
Is made out of two yellows.

Grounds for Recollection

(An old footballer remembers)

'Do you remember *Anfield*?' he asked.
Old Trafford nodded his head.
'She lived down near the *Maine Road*
By *St Andrew's* church,' he said.

'*Molineux* her too,' he said.
'They went to *St James's* school.
They once pretended to find a *Goldstone*.
They were always playing the fool.

'They tore down *The Shed* and built *The New Den*
In *The Dell* by *The Riverside*.
They used sticks they took from *The Hawthorns*
And *Turf* from the *Moor* inside.

'Once for a lark, in *Goodison Park*,
They made all of us boys go trembly
By claiming they'd found on the *City's Ground*
A Cup Final ticket for *Wembley*!'

NONSENSE FOOTBALL RHYMES

Doctor Selsey

Doctor Selsey went to Chelsea
In a shower of rain.
He felt so ill when they lost five-nil
That he never went there again.

Golden Boots

'Golden Boots, Golden Boots,
Where have you been?'
'I've been up to London
To visit the Queen.'

'Golden Boots, Golden Boots,
What did she say?'
'I saw you sent off
On Match of the Day!'

Old King Cole

Old King Cole scored a very fine goal,
A very fine goal scored he.
A TV poll reckoned King Cole's goal
Was the best you'd ever see.

The Price of Fame

It's not easy being famous.

Last week I was a hero.
In injury-time
my namesake scored the winner
with a glancing header.

Everyone ran round the playground,
chanting my name.

Today, I'm a villain.
Last night I missed an open goal.
Then, just after half-time,
I was sent off for a professional foul.
We lost two-nil.

Everyone's blaming me and calling me names.

If it goes on like this,
I'm going to ask Sir for a transfer.

Bullying
Poems

And How Was School Today?

Each day they ask: And how was school today?
Behind my mask, I shrug and say O.K.

Upstairs, alone, I blink away the tears
Hearing again their scornful jeers and sneers.

Hearing again them call me by those names
As they refused to let me join their games.

Feeling again them mock me with their glares
As they pushed past me rushing down the stairs.

What have I done? Why won't they let me in?
Why do they snigger? What's behind that grin?

Each day they ask: And how was school today?
Behind my mask, I shrug and say O.K.

Four O'clock Friday

Four o'clock Friday, I'm home at last.
Time to forget the week that's past.
On Monday, in break they stole my ball
And threw it over the playground wall.
On Tuesday afternoon, in games
They threw mud at me and called me names.
On Wednesday, they trampled my books on the floor,
So Miss kept me in because I swore.
On Thursday, they laughed after the test
'Cause my marks were lower than the rest.
Four o'clock Friday, at last I'm free,
For two whole days they can't get at me.

Why Won't They Talk to Me?

Why won't they talk to me?
Each day it's just the same.
No one will talk to me.
To them it's like a game.

When I walk into the room,
They turn their heads away.
No one will sit by me.
No one asks me to play.

What have I done to them?
Why do they pick on me?
What am I doing wrong?
Please someone, talk to me.

Walk Tall

'Walk tall,' Dad said. 'Hold up your head.
Don't ever let them see
you're scared.'

But there are four of them
and only one of me.

As I walk past, they turn and stare,
but I don't let them see
I'm scared.

'Cause there are four of them
and only one of me.

If You Want to Join the Gang

They said that I had to do it,
if I wanted to join the gang.
So I waited with them outside the school
when they picked on Tony Chang.

I was there when they jumped on him.
I was there when they ripped his shirt.
I was there when they emptied out his bag
and kicked his books in the dirt.

They said that I had to do it,
if I wanted to join their gang,
but now I feel bad that I was there
when they picked on Tony Chang.

I Feel Bad

I feel bad about Sharon.
I feel bad about what I did.
But when I saw them coming,
I ran away and hid.

I watched as they laughed and spat.
I watched as they made her cry.
I didn't stand up for her.
I didn't even try.

I feel bad about Sharon.
I feel bad about what I did.
But when I saw them coming,
I just ran away and hid.

If He Hits You

'If he hits you, hit him back.'
That's what my father said.
So I hit him and now I am
In trouble with the Head.

He hit me first. He started it.
I didn't want a fight.
Now I'm in trouble with the Head
and I don't think that's right.

If You Tell

'If you tell, we'll get you.'
That's what they always say.
So I give them what they want.
It's easier that way.

They take my things.
They break my things.
They know I'll never tell.
For telling tales just isn't done.
But not telling tales is hell.

It Hurts

It hurts when someone makes remarks
About the clothes I wear,
About the foods I refuse to eat
Or the way I cover my hair.

It hurts when someone laughs and jokes
About the way I speak.
'Ignore them,' says my Dad, but it's hard
To turn the other cheek.

It hurts when someone calls me names
Because of the colour of my skin.
Everyone's different outside,
But we're all the same within.

Half-term Holiday Daydreams

On Monday, I dreamed a bull
that chased Michael
across the playground
and tossed him over the fence
into a patch of nettles.

On Tuesday, I dreamed a giant
who stuck his hand
through the classroom window,
plucked Michael from his desk
and carried him off to toast for his tea.

On Wednesday, I dreamed a pirate
who kidnapped Michael
on his way to school,
tied him to the mast of his ship,
then made him walk the plank.

On Thursday, I dreamed a wizard,
who cast a spell on Michael,
as he barged to the front of the dinner queue,
turned him into a banana skin
and dropped him into the waste bucket.

On Friday, I dreamed an alien
that landed its spacecraft
on the roof of the hall,
dragged Michael out of assembly
and whisked him away to a distant planet.

On Saturday, I dreamed a dragon
that swooped over the recreation ground,
snatched Michael in its claws,
then flew off back to its cave
where it kept him a prisoner for ever.

On Sunday, I dreamed a ghost
that haunted Michael's bedroom,
waking him up with bloodcurdling screams
that made his teeth chatter
and turned his hair white.

On Monday morning, I went back.
There in the playground
were Michael and his mates
waiting for me, as usual.

I Was Bullied Once

I was bullied once.
Now I'm a bully too.
They took it out on me.
So I'll take it out on you.

War

Poems

'It Isn't Right to Fight'

You said, 'It isn't right to fight,'
But when we watched the news tonight,
You shook your fist and said
You wished the tyrant and his cronies dead.
When I asked why,
If it's not right to fight,
You gave a sigh,
You shook your head
And sadly said,
'Sometimes a cause is just
And, if there is no other way,
Perhaps, you must.'

Just Another War

On her sideboard
Nan has a picture
Of a young man
In a soldier's uniform
Smiling proudly.

'That's my brother,
Your Uncle Reg,'
She says,
Her voice tinged
With sadness.

'He was killed
In Korea.
He was only nineteen.'

'Where's Korea?' I say.
'What were they fighting for?'

'Somewhere in Asia,'
She says.
'I don't know.
It was just another war.'

WordSwords

(A wargame)

Play with words.
Make a sword.
Shift gear
Into rage.
Turn snug
Into guns.
Make raw
Make war:
Listen – enlist
Tool – loot.
Roses
Becomes sores,
While skill
Kills.

War Games

In a Star Wars T-shirt,
Armed with an Airfix bomber,
The young avenger
Crawls across the carpet
To blast the wastepaper basket
Into oblivion.

Later,
Curled on the sofa,
He watches unflinching
An edited version
Of War of the Day,
Only half-listening
As the newscaster
Lists the latest statistics.

Cushioned by distance
How can he comprehend
The real score?

Who's to Say?

*(On the fiftieth anniversary of the Battle of El Alamein,
October 1992)*

Great-grandmother said,
'Fifty years ago today,
your great-grandfather was killed.
They say it was the battle
that turned the tide of the war –
the first great Allied victory.
Ten thousand of our young men died.
They calculated the sacrifice was worth it.
Who's to say?
All I know is,
if there had been no war,
he might still be here
today.'

Suicide Bombers

(July 2005)

When religious anger
fuels the mind
then you will find
some people so blind
that they are willing
to sacrifice themselves
on the altar of killing.

TV Wars

(1991 version)

We sat in our living-rooms and watched
With a mixture of awe and pride
As the bombs poured from the sky
And Iraqi soldiers died.

We sat in our living-rooms and watched
The scenes on the mountainside
With a mixture of horror and guilt
As Kurdish families died.

We sat in our living-rooms and watched,
Feeling powerless we sighed,
As the Serbian troops advanced
And Croatian people died.

We sat in our living-rooms and watched.
'What else can we do?' we cried.
As we silently wrote out cheques,
Passing by on the other side.

I Saw It On the News, Daddy

'I saw it on the news, Daddy.
There was a man with a gun.
Why did he shoot the little girl?
What had she done?'

'She hadn't done anything.
She happened to be in that place.
When the angry man started shooting –
The man from a different race.'

'She was just a little girl, Daddy.
Why did she have to die?
Daddy, I don't understand.'
'Child, neither do I.'

Goran

At the end of science,
No one could find Goran,
The new kid from Sarajevo.

Eventually, someone heard a sobbing
Coming from a cupboard
At the back of the room.

Miss opened the door
And there was Goran
Curled up inside.

Miss coaxed him out
And put her arm round him.

We filed quietly out to play,
Wondering what nightmares
The flames from our Bunsen burners
Had sparked inside
His war-scarred mind.

Market Forces
(The arms dealer's defence)

We sold the guns
but we didn't know
where the guns
were going to go.

We didn't know.
Why should we care?
We needed to sell
the guns somewhere.

We sold the guns.
What's the fuss?
Someone wanted them.
Don't blame us!

The Bosnian Question

(July 1995)

When racial hate
divides a state
and people fight,
is it right
for those outside
simply to watch
the genocide
and wait
for thousands more
to meet their fate?

They Have Blown My Legs Away

They have blown my legs away.
They have cut my life in half.
The men who planted the mines
Say they acted on my behalf.

It doesn't really matter
What they were fighting for.
It's innocent people like me
Who pay the price of their war.

But it's people half a world away
Who should hang their heads in shame –
The people who made and sold the toys
That they use in their wicked game.

I Woke With a Fright

I woke with a fright
In the middle of the night
At the sound of drunken singing.
Outside in the street
I heard tramping feet
Then the telephone started ringing.

When I picked up the phone
I heard someone groan
And give a deep sigh of despair.
There was no reply
But a tortured cry
When I asked: ' Who's there? Who's there?'

Then I heard glass smash
And a thundering crash
Of fists as they hammered the door.
Someone shouted: 'Stand back!'
I heard a gun crack
And I fell to my knees on the floor.

I Dream of a Time

I dream of a time

When the only blades are blades of corn
When the only barrels are barrels of wine
When the only tanks are full of water
When the only chains are chains of hands

I hope for a time…

Paying His Respects

Great-Grandad never talked
About the war.
'That,' he'd say with a sigh,
'That's over and done with.'

When I asked him
If the war was like the wars
In comics and in films,
He simply said,
'No, it was real.'

Every year
He got out his medals
And joined the parade
To the cenotaph,
Paying his respects.

Poems About Our World

All Things Dry and Dusty

All things dry and dusty,
All plants shrivelled and small,
All trees bare and blighted,
It's man who made them all.

The shoots that twist and wither.
The rotten leaves that fall,
The fruits that do not ripen,
It's man who made them all.

All things dry and dusty,
All plants shrivelled and small,
All trees bare and blighted,
It's man who made them all.

The fields that yield no harvest,
The empty market stall,
The orchard's fruitless trees,
It's man who made them all.

All things dry and dusty,
All plants shrivelled and small,
All trees bare and blighted,
It's man who made them all.

Graveyard Scene

There are no names on the gravestones now,
They've been washed away by the rain.
The graveyard trees are skeletons now,
They will never wear leaves again.

Instead of a forest, the tower surveys
A bleak and desolate plain.
Those are not tears in the gargoyle's eyes,
They are droplets of acid rain.

Beneath the Bridge

Once, when Gran was a girl,
A river flowed
Between these banks
Its waters fresh and clear.

Now, the river bed
Is dried and cracked.
No water flows.
Instead,
Beneath the bridge,
A dirt-stained mattress
Leaks its stuffing
And plastic bags
Spew pools of rubbish.

Over the bridge,
Where Gran stood throwing sticks
Into the swirling current,
A stream of traffic roars,
Oblivious.

Pretty Lady Wrapped in Fur

Pretty lady wrapped in fur
Do you not care
About the squirrels
Whose coats you wear?

The Price

There's a price for the eggs you eat,
It's the hens that have to pay,
Locked in their battery cages
Day after day after day.

'It's warm and dry,' the farmer says,
'There's plenty to drink and eat.'
But the sloping wire-mesh floor
Gives them deformed feet.

There's nowhere for them to perch.
It's hard to turn around.
They cannot spread their wings
Or forage for food on the ground.

'The profit margin's higher,'
I heard the farmer say.
'It's in everybody's interest
To keep the hens this way.'

There's a price for the eggs you eat,
It's the hens that have to pay,
Locked in their battery cages
Day after day after day.

Standing on the Hilltop

On Sunday morning
We woke at first light
And climbed the hill behind the campsite
Before breakfast.
Standing in the crisp morning air,
Looking out across the moorland,
Watching the clear water of the stream
As it tumbled over the stones,
The world and all its problems
Seemed a world away.

The Recycling Rap

Listen to me children. Hear what I say.
We've got to start recycling. It's the only way
To save this planet for future generations –
The name of the game is reclamation.
You've got to start recycling. You know it makes sense.
You've got to start recycling. Stop sitting on the fence.
No more pussyfooting. No more claptrap.
Get yourself doing the recycling rap.

Come on and start recycling. Start today
By saving old newspapers, not throwing them away.
Don't just take them and dump them on the tip,
Tie them in a bundle and put them in the skip.

Get collecting, protecting the future's up to you.
Save all your old glass bottles and your jamjars too.
Take them to the bottle bank, then at the factory
The glass can be recycled, saving energy.

Don't chuck away that empty drink can.
Remember what I said. Start recycling, man.
Wash it, squash it, squeeze it flat and thin.
Take it to the Save-A-Can and post it in.

Listen to me children. Hear what I say.
We've got to start recycling. It's the only way
To save this planet for future generations –
The name of the game is reclamation.
You've got to start recycling. You know it makes sense.
You've got to start recycling. Stop sitting on the fence.
No more pussyfooting. No more claptrap.
Get yourself doing the recycling rap.

Modified Progress

They bred the seed. They fed the seed.
They nurtured it with care.
They promised a bumper harvest
For all the world to share.

They piled it high upon the shelves.
It glowed with health outside.
But who knows where the changes stop
When crops are modified?

Where Is the Forest?

Where is the forest?
cried the animals.
Where are the trees?

We needed the wood,
said the people.
Wood to make fires.
Wood to build houses.
We cut it down.

Where is the forest?
cried the animals.
Where are the trees?

We needed the land,
said the people.
Land for our cattle.
Land for our roads.
We cut it down.

Where is the forest?
cried the animals.
Where is our home?

Gone, whispered the wind.
Gone. Gone. Gone.

The African Farmer's Song

The sun is fierce and hot.
The earth is hard and dry.
Day after day, no rain falls
Out of a cloudless sky.

Oh, bring us some water!
Bring us some rain!
So our fields can all
Grow green again.

The water-hole is empty.
The stream is no longer flowing.
There are no leaves on the trees.
The crops have all stopped growing.

Oh, bring us some water!
Bring us some rain!
So our fields can all
Grow green again.

Olympic Circles

While they circled the track,
Muscles straining, lungs bursting,
In search of gold,
Elsewhere, lips cracked, stomachs knotted,
Others trudged under the same sun
In search of food,
While overhead the vultures circled.

Sitting in the Doorway

Sitting in the doorway
With nothing to eat,
Feeling the cold
Biting my feet.

Sitting in the doorway
With nothing to do,
At the back of the line –
The end of the queue.

Sitting in the doorway
With nowhere to hide
From the night's bitter chill
And the hunger inside.

Sitting in the doorway
With nothing.

Standing on the Sidelines

I'm standing on the sidelines,
Practising with a ball,
Developing my skills,
Waiting for your call.

I'm standing on the sidelines,
Waving at each train,
Wondering if, and when or where
I'll catch a ride again.

I'm standing in the courtroom,
Accused of the crime
Of trying to scrape a living
While idly killing time.

I'm standing in the corridor.
I'm waiting in the queue.
I'd rather not be here.
But it's what I have to do.

Immigration Trap

Farida's mum is being sent home.
But Farida's allowed to stay.
Farida doesn't want her to go
But Farida doesn't have a say.

Farida's lived here all her life.
She's British, like you and me.
But Farida's mum came here
As a stateless refugee.

And now the people who make the rules
Say Farida's mum must go
Back to the land she left
Twelve long years ago.

Back to a troubled land
Where people live in fear.
She has outstayed her welcome.
She is not wanted here.

But because Farida was born here,
Farida's allowed to stay.
She doesn't want her mum to go,
But she doesn't have a say.

One of the Many

No more waiting for the knock on the door.
No more crouching on the cellar floor.

No more listening to the T.V. lies.
No more disguising the look in your eyes.

No more watching what you say on the phone.
No more the feeling that you're never alone.

No more editing every word that you say.
No more curfew at the end of each day.

No more censoring what you're able to know.
No more following wherever you go.

No more being told what to think, what to do,
Except to stand here, to wait in the queue –

One of the many, not one of the few,
A free refugee.

Christmas Wishes

If I had three Christmas wishes
My first wish would be
For an end to hunger and poverty.

If I had three Christmas wishes
My second would be for
An end to violence, hatred and war.

If I had three Christmas wishes
My third wish would be
That we take proper care of the land and the sea.

Weather Poems

It's Raining Cats and Dogs

MUM: It's raining cats and dogs out there.

GRAN: The dog's out where?

MUM: No, it's raining very hard.
It's very wet out.

GRAN: The vet's come out.
Why? Is the dog not well.

MUM: The dog's fine.

GRAN: No, it's not.
It's raining cats and dogs.

The Lake

On a calm day
The lake
Imagines it is a mirror
And smiles back
At people who pass by
Smiling.

On a breezy day
The lake
Hunches its shoulders
And sends ripples
Scudding across the surface.

On a winter's day
The lake
Hides itself
Under a frozen blanket
And refuses to budge
Until it is warm enough
To come out again.

The Wild Wind

Sweeping down the street,
Swerving through the trees,
Snatching leaves and twigs
To whisk in its breeze.

Whistling round the chimneys,
Whooshing under floors,
Sniffing at the windows,
Snapping shut the doors.

Shattering the silence
Wherever it goes,
Swirling, twirling, whirling,
The wild wind blows.

When the Wind Blows

When the wind blows
Coats flap, scarves flutter.

When the wind blows
Branches groan, leaves mutter.

When the wind blows
Curtains swish, papers scatter.

When the wind blows
Gates creak, dustbins clatter.

When the wind blows
Doors slam, windows rattle.

When the wind blows
Inside is a haven,
Outside is a battle.

Winds

The spring wind
Is a bouncy breeze
Coaxing seeds and shoots,
Showering promises of summer.

The summer wind
Is a parched sigh
Rustling wheatfields,
Stirring up dust.

The autumn wind
Is a mischievous thief
Whistling cheerfully,
Scattering leaves with abandon.

The winter wind
Is an icicle wind
Knifing through bark,
Chilling to the bone.

Summer Storm

Light travels, said Miss,
Faster than sound.
Next time there's a storm,
When you see the lightning,
Start counting slowly in seconds.
If you divide
The number of seconds by three,
It will tell you
How many kilometres you are
From the centre of the storm.

Two nights later,
I was woken
By the lashing rain,
The lightning,
And the thunder's crash.

I lay,
Huddled beneath the sheet,
As the rain poured down
And lightning lit up the bedroom,
Slowly counting the seconds,
Listening for the thunder
And calculating the distance
As the storm closed in –

Until,
With a blinding flash
And a simultaneous ear-splitting crash,
The storm passed
Directly overhead.

And I shook with fright
As the storm passed on,
Leaving the branches shuddering
And the leaves weeping.

Facts About Air

Scientists say
That air consists
Of about 78% nitrogen and 21% oxygen,
Plus some carbon dioxide
And small amounts
Of the rare gases – helium, argon and neon.

These are facts, I know.
But I also know
That when I go outside
On a spring morning
The air tastes as crisp
As a fresh lettuce
And that when I sit
On the patio
On a summer evening
The cool night air
Brushes my cheeks like a feather.

Gathering Storm

The bright sunlight disappeared
Behind an angry cloud.
The birdsong faltered.
Caught in gusts of wind
Leaves shivered, branches groaned.
The scudding sky loured.
I shuddered
As the day changed its face.

What Is Fog?

Puffs of dragon smoke
Curling round hedges and trees.

Clouds of steam from a giant's kettle
Pouring out over the city.

The breath from a dinosaur's nostrils
Blurring the world into a grey shadow.

Heatwave

All day
the choking heat
made us wilt.

At night
we lay gasping
in the still air
like stranded fish.

Towards dawn
we fell into a fitful slumber,
only to be awoken
by the sun's fierce rays
heralding another scorcher.

Cold Snap

All day
the searing cold
numbed our bones.

At night
we lay huddled
under thick blankets,
cocooned against the cold.

Towards dawn
we awoke
and crept shivering
from our burrow
to brave another bitter day.

Last Night It Froze

There are ferns of frost on the window pane
And ice on the puddles in the lane.

Tufts of grass stick up like spikes.
It's far too slippery to ride our bikes.

Icicles hang like spears from the gutters.
The car engine whines and coughs and splutters.

The leaves on the trees are stiff and white.
While we slept, it froze last night.

The Snow Monster

When the Snow Monster sneezes,
Flurries of snow swirl and whirl,
Twisting round trees, curling into crevices,
Brushing the ground a brilliant white.

When the Snow Monster bellows,
Blizzards blot out the sky,
Piling up drifts, blocking roads,
Burying the landscape in a white grave.

When the Snow Monster cries,
Soft flakes slip and slide gently down
Into the hands of waiting children
Who test their taste with their tongues.

When the Snow Monster sleeps,
The air crackles with children's laughter
As they throw snowballs, build snowmen
And whiz downhill on their sledges.

Thaw

Overnight, the garden's
White carpet has disappeared.
Now, the lawn is bare.
The trees stand like skeletons.
The magic has melted away.

Seasons
Poems

It's Spring

It's spring
And the garden is changing its clothes,
Putting away
Its dark winter suits,
Its dull scarves
And drab brown overcoats.

Now, it wraps itself in green shoots,
Slips on blouses
Sleeved with pink and white blossom,
Pulls on skirts of daffodil and primrose,
Snowdrop socks and purple crocus shoes,
Then dances in the sunlight.

There's a Spring in Your Step

There's a spring in your step
    as you march into April
and the daffodils nod in the breeze.
There's a spring in your step
    as you march into April
and the blossom brightens the trees.

There's a spring in your step
    as you march into April
and the lambs gambol on the grass.
There's a spring in your step
    as you march into April
and winter fades away as you pass.

There's a spring in your step
    as you march into April
and the sun climbs higher in the sky.
There's a spring in your step
    as you march into April
and you wave dreary winter goodbye.

Spring Snow

(A cinquain)

Snowflakes
Slip from the sky
Like soft white butterflies,
Brush the trees with their flimsy wings,
Vanish.

Spring Haiku

Pale lemon primroses
Whispering promises of summer
On a dull March day.

Swaying in the breeze,
Their heads nodding, bluebells ring,
Heralding summer.

Golden daffodils
Trumpeting triumphantly
Proclaim: Spring is here!

Summer

Summer wakes early.
The sun is her alarm clock.
She is washed and dressed
And out in the garden long before breakfast.
She bustles about all morning
Fussing over her flowers.
At noon, she straightens her back,
Acknowledges the sun with a wave,
Then bends once more
To spend the long afternoon and early evening
Tending her precious plants.
At twilight, she casts a quick glance
To assure herself
All's well with her charges,
Then hurries off
To snatch a few hours' sleep
Before the sun rouses her again.

Summer Clouds

Fluffy white clouds
Their sails billowing
Chase each other
Across the blue of the sky
Playfully.

Dark thunder clouds –
A battalion on stand-by –
Mass on the horizon
Menacingly.

Wispy white clouds
Like seagulls' feathers
Drift high in the sky
Lazily.

Recipe for a Summer Holiday

Take a stretch of sandy beach
and a calm sea.
Add a pier, a promenade,
donkey-rides and a fun-fair.
Sprinkle with buckets and spades,
deck-chairs, lilos and picnic baskets.
Cover with warm slices of sunshine
and wrap in warm photographs
to look at on dark winter days.

Sand

Sand in your fingernails
Sand between your toes
Sand in your earholes
Sand up your nose!

Sand in your sandwiches
Sand on your bananas
Sand in your bed at night
Sand in your pyjamas!

Sand in your sandals
Sand in your hair
Sand in your knickers
Sand everywhere!

Sand Writing

We wrote with a stick on the sand:
PATRICIA AND SUSAN WERE HERE.
Then we stood and watched like Canute
As the waves made the words disappear.

Autumn News Bulletin

Today, the trees are in shock.
Overnight, a sustained assault
Has left them battered and bare.
There are leaves everywhere –
On roads and pathways,
Scattered on lawns and flowerbeds,
Clustered in doorways
And the corners of buildings.

In some gardens
Men with rakes have appeared.
In due course, barrow loads of leaves
Will be heaped into bonfires.
Now, in the aftermath of the storm,
There is an air of resignation.
As one of the residents put it:
'I suppose it's to be expected.
It happens every year.'

November

November is a grey road
Cloaked in mist.
A twist of wood-smoke
In the gathering gloom.
A scurrying squirrel
Hoarding acorns.
A steel-grey river
Glinting in the twilight.
A grey rope
Knotted around a threadbare tree.

December Day

December day

       the ground
       brittle with frost
       crunches
       beneath your feet.

Trees

       shorn of their leaves
       shiver
       in the thin wind
       thrusting their branches
       defiantly
       skywards

       while their roots dig deeper

       seeking succour in the soil

Winter Trees

(a triolet)

The winter trees
In falling snow
Shiver and freeze.
The winter trees
Bow in the breeze,
Branches bent low:
The winter trees
In falling snow.

Winter

Whirling snow and whistling wind
Icy patterns on window panes
Numb fingers and freezing toes
Trees stripped bare
Earth bone-hard
Roaring fires and long, dark nights.

Hard Winters

Outside
The bare branches of trees
Shiver in the wind
And the frozen grass
Sticks up like spikes
From the hard ground.

Inside
Children with chapped hands
Stretch thin fingers
To catch wisps of warmth
From scraps of coal
Glimmering in the iron grate.

Giant Winter

Giant Winter preys on the earth,
Gripping with talons of ice,
Squeezing, seeking a submission,
Tightening his grip like a vice.

Starved of sunlight, shivering trees
Are bent by his torturing breath.
The seeds burrow into the soil
Preparing to fight to the death.

Giant Winter sneers at their struggles,
Blows blizzards from his frozen jaws,
Ripples cold muscles of iron,
Clenches tighter his icicle claws.

Just as he seems to be winning,
Strength suddenly ebbs from his veins.
He releases his hold and collapses.
Giant Spring gently takes up the reins.

Snarling, bitter with resentment,
Winter crawls to his polar den,
Where he watches and waits till it's time
To renew the battle again.

Animal
Poems

It's a Dog's Life

Mum says
Our dog's
Having an identity crisis.

Yesterday,
He went out into the garden,
Then tried to come back in
Through the cat flap.

He jammed his head so tight,
No matter how hard
We pushed and pulled
It wouldn't budge.

In the end,
We had to call the fire brigade.

When Dad came home
He nearly had a fit,
When he saw
What they'd done to the door.

He called the dog
All sorts of names.
But when the dog jumped up
To beg for his evening walk,
Dad still took him.

It's not fair.
If I'd smashed the door,
I wouldn't have been allowed out
For at least two weeks!

The Guard Dog

I'm a gruff dog, a rough dog,
I'm good in a fight.
Keep your distance
Or I might bite.

I'm a mean dog, a keen dog,
I'm quick on my paws.
Stand well back
From my vicious jaws.

I'm a proud dog, a loud dog,
Hear me growl.
One false move
And I'll make you howl.

I'm a hard dog, a guard dog,
A dog to fear.
You have been warned.
Don't come near!

Cats

Fat cat lies
By the living room fire.

Fat cat yawns.
Fat cat stirs.

Fat cat stretches.
Fat cat purrs.

Thin cat slinks
By the garden fence.

Thin cat's eyes
Are narrow slits.

Thin cat hisses.
Thin cat spits.

Mrs Nugent's Budgie

Yesterday,
Our neighbour Mrs Nugent
Accidentally sat on her budgie.
'How did it happen?' I asked.
'Was it flattened?' said Sally.
'Like on Tom and Jerry.'
'She'd let it out
For a fly around,' said Mum.
'And she sat down on the bed
Without noticing it was there.'
'Poor thing,' said Dad.
'It didn't stand much of a chance
With her on top of it.'
'It's not dead!' said Mum.
'It lay there stunned for a while,
Then started to twitch.
So she picked it up
And popped it back in its cage.
It looked fine when I saw it,
Except that its head
Is a bit on one side.'
'Will it be all right?' I asked.
'I expect so,' said Dad.
'It sounds a tough old bird,
Like Mrs Nugent!'

The Invaders

Today it is snowing.
The starlings are out in force
Bullying the sparrows,
Their bayonet beaks
Commandeering the breadcrumbs.
Like stormtroopers
They take over the garden,
Asserting that might means right.

Kingfisher

Dropping
Like a splinter from the sky
It knives the water,
Swiftly strikes,
Turns, surges
Up through the splattering surface,
Back to the willow branch,
Where it sits triumphant,
Wet feathers glistening,
Its silver catch
Dangling from its beak.

BIRD TALK

Percy the Parrot

I'm Percy the Parrot.
If you didn't want me to comment,
Why did you teach me to talk?
I can swear like a trooper
Or bid you 'Good morning'
As politely as any butler.
The choice is yours.
The choice is yours.
The choice is yours.

Smith the Sparrow

I'm Smith the Sparrow.
Common or garden, that's me.
The bird in the street.
I know my place.
The window-ledge or the gutter,
It's all the same to me.
I'm no high-flier,
Just one of the many,
Picking up the crumbs,
Taking life as it comes.

Mr Vulture

I'm Mr Vulture,
Happy to be of service,
When there's a carcass needs disposing.
Why am I still circling?
Just biding my time.
I didn't mean to offend you
When I said,
'I've a bone to pick with you.'

In the Still Dark

In the still dark,
High above the meadow,
The barn owl hovers,
Ear flaps erect,
Listening.

In the still dark,
Down in the meadow,
The small brown fieldmouse
Crunches the corn husk,
Unsuspecting.

In the still dark,
High above the meadow,
The barn owl swivels,
With deadly precision
Pinpointing its prey.

In the still dark,
Down towards the meadow,
The barn owl
Plunges silently,
Talons outstretched.

In the still dark,
Down in the meadow,
The barn owl
Strikes.

The Brown Bear

In winter,
When the cold winds blow,
When the land
Is covered with snow
The brown bear sleeps.

In winter,
When the nights come soon,
When the land
Freezes beneath the moon
The brown bear dreams.

The brown bear
Dreams of summer heat,
Of berries,
Honey and nuts to eat.
The brown bear sighs.

The brown bear
Stirs, then digs down deep,
Safe and sound
In its winter sleep.
The brown bear dreams.

Giraffe

Giraffe,
Sometimes
You make me laugh
Way up there
In the skies.

But when
You stoop
To stare at me,
You cut me
Down to size.

The New Gnus

A gnu who was new to the zoo
Asked another gnu what he should do.
The other gnu said, shaking his head,
'If I knew, I'd tell you. I'm new too!'

The Llama

The llama is a charmer.
He'll take you by surprise.
He'll pull the wool
Over anyone's eyes.

The Crocodile

The crocodile has a toothy smile.
He opens his jaws with a grin.
He's very polite.
Before taking a bite
He always says, 'Please come in!'

Kangaroo

Approach with care the kangaroo,
Whose most distinguishing feature
Is that he is easily spooked:
He is a jumpy creature!

Farm Animals Haiku

Scattered like boulders
Across the moorland – grey sheep
Grazing the sparse grass.

Sniffing and snuffling
Mud-spattered pigs search the trough
For scraps and scrapings.

The black and white cow
Stares glass-eyed, switches its tail,
Chews contentedly.

Insects

Insects creep,
Insects crawl,
Insects drive you up the wall.

Insects tickle,
Insects bite,
Insects get you in the night.

Insects nibble,
Insects nip,
Insects suck and insects sip.

Insects breed,
Insects hatch,
Insects make you scratch, scratch, scratch.

Insects here,
Insects there,
Insects in your underwear.

Insects creep,
Insects crawl,
Insects drive me up the wall.

The Bedbug's Story

'When I was young and handsome,'
The ancient bedbug said,
'I lived in a royal palace
And slept in a royal bed.

'They called me the most fearless
Bug that has ever been.
I'm the bug that bit the bottoms
Of the king and of the queen!'

Dinosaur
and
Dragon
Poems

Ten Dancing Dinosaurs

Ten dancing dinosaurs in a chorus line
One fell and split her skirt, then there were nine.

Nine dancing dinosaurs at a village fête
One was raffled as a prize, then there were eight.

Eight dancing dinosaurs on a pier in Devon
One fell overboard, then there were seven.

Seven dancing dinosaurs performing magic tricks
One did a vanishing act, then there were six.

Six dancing dinosaurs learning how to jive
One got twisted in a knot, then there were five.

Five dancing dinosaurs gyrating on the floor
One crashed through the floorboards,
    then there were four.

Four dancing dinosaurs waltzing in the sea
A mermaid kidnapped one, then there were three.

Three dancing dinosaurs head-banging in a zoo
One knocked himself out, then there were two.

Two dancing dinosaurs rocking round the sun
One collapsed from sunstroke, then there was one.

One dancing dinosaur climbed aboard a plane,
Flew off to Alaska and was never seen again!

We've a Pet Pterodactyl

We've a pet pterodactyl.
We keep it in the attic.
When it flaps its wings
It makes an awful racket.

We've a pet pterodactyl.
We've locked it in a cage.
It squawks and it screeches.
It's always in a rage.

Don't get a pterodactyl
And keep it as a pet.
It bites you when you feed it.
It even bit the vet!

We've a pet pterodactyl.
We'd really like to sell it.
But no one wants to buy it.
Who can blame them once they smell it!

Why the Dinosaurs Became Extinct

The reason for the extinction
Of the whole of the dinosaur race
Is that one day the Earth began spinning so fast
They were all flung off into space.

'I'm Bored,' Said Young Dragon

'I'm bored,' said young dragon,
'There's nothing to do.
The knights have all run away.
There's nothing to watch on the telly
And no one will come out to play.'

'Why don't you practise your roaring
Or revise for the fire-breathing test?
Or lie on your ledge at the back of the cave,
Read your book and have a good rest?'

'I'm not doing that! That's boring!'
Said young dragon, scratching the floor.
'Stop doing that!' roared his mother.
'You'll get dirt all over your claw.'

'I'm bored,' said young dragon,
'There's nothing to do.'
And he started to pick at a scale.
'Stop doing that!' roared his mother
And she gave him a flick with her tail.

'I'm bored,' said young dragon.
'There are no knights to fight.
Why can't I go out for a fly?
I'll watch out for planes and I promise
I won't fly too high in the sky.'

'Oh, all right,' said his mother, patting his wings,
'But listen carefully to me.
Don't you go near that castle
And be back here in time for your tea.'

Interview with a Dragon

What's your name?

Firesnorter.
I'm Thunderflash and Firecracker's daughter.

Where were you born?

In Stalactite Cavern,
High on the hill above Flamethrowers Tavern.

What games do you like playing?

Maiden-chasing. Fight-a-Knight
And Try to Set the Torch Alight.

Which football team do you support?

Cave City Rovers – the best team by far
With Toaster, their ten-million goalscoring star.

What are your favourite foods?

Mammoth and chips and roasted boggart
And ten-litre buckets of gorse-flavoured yoghurt.

What are your favourite drinks?

Hot gearbox oil. Runny boiling custard
And five-star petrol spiced with mustard.

What are your favourite films?

The Last Crusader.
Knights on Fire and *The Scorched Invader.*

What are your hobbies?

Collecting treasure. Painting caves.
Stealing princesses as slaves.

What is your ambition?

To set the world on fire.
To conquer knights.
To see my name up there in lights.

At the School For Young Dragons

At the school for young dragons
The main lessons are
Flying and feasting and fighting.

In flying they learn
How to take off and land
How to dive and to swoop
How to loop the loop
And how to leave trails of sky-writing.

In feasting they learn
About how to behave
When invited to dine
In an old dragon's cave.
They learn that it's rude
To gobble your food,
That you should not belch fire
That you must always sit up straight
And never, ever, scorch your plate.

In fighting they learn
How to scare off their foes
With jets of flame
That will singe their toes,
How to puff a smoke screen
So they cannot be seen.
How a knight with a lance
Hasn't much of a chance
Against dragons who know
How a whack of the tail
Can shatter chain-mail.

At the school for young dragons
The main lessons are
Flying and feasting and fighting,
Which is why you will hear
A young dragon say
'Our lessons are really exciting!
It's better than reading and writing!'

Sky-Dragon

I am Sky-Dragon,
Lord of the thunder.
When I bellow and roar,
Clouds tear asunder.

When I raise my claw,
The pouring rain
Cascades from the sky
Flooding valley and plain.

When I lash my tail,
The howling gales
Snap the masts of ships
And shred their sails.

When I breathe my fire,
Zigzag stripes
Flash through the sky
As the lightning strikes.

I am Sky-Dragon,
When you hear me roar,
Fasten your windows
And bolt the door!

The Dragon-Diner

I'm a twenty-first century dragon,
I run the Dragon-Diner.
If it's fast-food that you want,
You won't find any finer.

With a flick of the flame
From my fiery lips
I can sizzle you up
A steak and chips.

Beefburgers, bacon,
Crisp, crunchy fish,
Potato cakes, ham and eggs,
Name your dish!

I'm faster than a microwave.
There's no food finer.
If it's fast-food that you want,
Come to the Dragon-Diner.

The Fire Monster

Deep in the boiling belly
Of the volcano
The Fire Monster sleeps:
Wisps of smoke from his nostrils
Squeeze through cracks
In the crater's mouth.

Deep in the boiling belly
Of the volcano
The Fire Monster stirs:
Bubbles of lava from his lips
Foam through crevices
And simmer beneath the surface.

Deep in the boiling belly
Of the volcano
The Fire Monster wakes:
Jets of lava gush from his throat,
Squirting through fissures,
Bursting the crater's dam.

Deep in the boiling belly
Of the volcano
The Fire Monster roars:
Huge chunks of rock spit from his mouth.
Red torrents of lava shoot into the sky
To stream down the crater's sides.

In the village in the valley,
The watchers wait
For the Fire Monster's anger to abate.

Chinese New Year Dragon

There's a brightly coloured dragon
Swaying down the street,
Stomping and stamping
And kicking up its feet.

There's a multi-coloured dragon –
Green, gold and red –
Twisting and twirling
And shaking its head.

There's a silky-scaled dragon
Parading through the town,
Swishing and swooshing
And rippling up and down.

There's a swirling, whirling dragon,
Weaving to and fro,
Prancing and dancing
And putting on a show.

There's cheering and clapping
As the dragon draws near –
A sign of good luck
And a happy New Year!

Wizard,
Ghost,
and
Vampire

Poems

The Mad Magician

In a dark and dingy dungeon
The Mad Magician dwells,
Mixing poisonous potions,
Concocting evil spells.

Into his bubbling cauldron
The Mad Magician throws
Handfuls of wriggling maggots,
The eyes of two dead crows,

The bladder of a nanny goat,
The snout of a year-old pig,
An eagle's claw, a vampire's tooth,
Hairs plucked from a judge's wig.

He waves his wicked wizard's wand.
He utters a piercing cry.
From their lairs, deep in the earth,
A thousand demons fly.

In a dark and dingy dungeon
The Mad Magician dwells,
Mixing poisonous potions,
Concocting evil spells.

The Hour When the Witches Fly

When the night is as cold as stone,
When lightning severs the sky,
When your blood is chilled to the bone,
That's the hour when the witches fly.

When the night-owl swoops for the kill,
When there's death in the fox's eye,
When the snake is coiled and still,
That's the hour when the witches fly.

When the nightmares scream in your head,
When you hear a strangled cry,
When you startle awake in your bed,
That's the hour when the witches fly.

When the sweat collects on your brow,
When the minutes tick slowly by,
When you wish it was then not now,
That's the hour when the witches fly.

Love Letter – from the Wizard to the Witch

I find your looks bewitching,
The way you stand and glare.
I love the way you shake your locks
Of tangled, matted hair.

I find your smile enchanting,
Your wicked, evil grin.
It makes me want to touch and stroke
Your gnarled and wrinkled skin.

I find your face spellbinding,
The warts upon your cheek,
So hairy, black and crusty –
They make my knees go weak.

I find you so enthralling.
I love your witchy smell
Of rats and dung and sewers –
You hold me in your spell!

The Ghost House

Don't go near the Ghost House. Don't go near!
Don't go near the Ghost House or you will hear:

The flutter of bats
Flitter flutter flitter flutter
The scratching of rats
Scritch scratch scritch scratch

Don't go near the Ghost House. Don't go near!
Don't go near the Ghost House or you will hear:

The clank of a chain
Clank CLANK KERLANK!
A cry of pain
Argh! ARGH! AARRGGHH!

Don't go near the Ghost House. Don't go near!
Don't go near the Ghost House or you will hear:

The rattle of bones
Rittle rattle rittle rattle
The moaning of moans
Moan MoAN MOAN!
The groaning of groans
Groan GroAN GROAN!

Don't go near the Ghost House. Don't you dare!
The Ghost House is a ghost house
'Cause the Ghost House isn't there!

The Shadow Man

At night-time
As I climb the stair
I tell myself
There's nobody there.

But what if there is?
What if he's there?
The Shadow Man
At the top of the stair.

What if he's lurking
There in the gloom
Of the landing
Right outside my room?

The Shadow Man
Who's so hard to see.
What if he's up there
Waiting for me?

At night-time
As I climb the stair
I tell myself
There's nobody there.

The Old House

The old house stands at the foot of the hill –
Blackened, silent, still.

They say on dark nights
You can hear
The ghost of a laugh
A cry of fear.

That you can see
Beside the wall
A shadowy figure
Gaunt and tall,
Clutching a bundle
Wrapped in a cloak.

That you can see
The swirling smoke
And hear the crackling
Of the fire
And watch as the flames
Leap higher and higher.

The old house stands at the foot of the hill –
Blackened, silent, still.

Who's Afraid?

Do I have to go haunting tonight?
The children might give me a fright.
It's dark in that house.
I might meet a mouse.
Do I have to go haunting tonight?

I don't like the way they scream out,
When they see me drifting about.
I'd much rather stay here,
Where there's nothing to fear.
Do I have to go haunting tonight?

The Magician's Ghost

The ghost of the magician said,
'I'm really in a fix.
The trouble is the audience
Sees right through all my tricks.'

Riddle Me a Count

My first is in blood and twice in undead.
My second is in nightmare and also in dread.
My third is in fangs but is not in doom.
My fourth is in coffin but not in tomb.
My fifth's in bloodsucker but not in vein.
My sixth's in bloodcurdling, and in bloodstain.
My last is in vampire but not in bite.
I rise from my grave on the stroke of midnight!

When Dracula Went to the Dentist

When Dracula went to the dentist,
The dentist smiled and said,
'There is nothing wrong with your teeth
Except for these specks of red.

'I wish that I had teeth like yours,'
Said the dentist brushing away.
'They're the finest set of teeth
I've seen for many a day.'

'You too can have a set like mine,'
Smiled Dracula. 'Here's my cheque.
Just pay it in at the blood bank
Along with those drops from your neck.'

The Vampire's Apology

'I didn't mean to cause offence,'
Said the vampire with a grin.
'But when I saw you'd cut your face,
I just had to lick your chin!'

A Late Night Drink

'A nightcap, sir?' the butler asked.
'A little drop of red?'
Dracula smiled and bared his teeth,
'If you don't mind,' he said.
'I always like a little nip,
Before I go to bed!'

The Friendly Vampire

'Come in,' the friendly vampire said.
'There's room in my tomb for two.
Together we'll have a late-night bite
And I'll share my drink with you!'

The man shook his head.
'I'd rather be dead!'
The vampire gave a grin.
He took a peck
At the poor man's neck
And greedily sucked him in.

Books to Make You Shudder and Shake

Coffins – The Inside Story by A. Deadbody
The Decapitated Ghost by Ed Underisarm
The Mummy in the Tomb by M. Balmer
The Vampire Is Coming by I.C. Dracula
How to Cook Human Flesh by B.A. Cannibal
Suffocated By Spiders by Ida Nightmare
Ghosts of the Marshlands by Jack O'Lantern
The Man Who Howled at the Full Moon
    by Izzie A. Werewolf
Disembodied Spirits by Esau Zombies
Entombed in the Dungeon by U.R. Doomed

The Frightening Phantom

Deep in the Forest of Fear
The Frightening Phantom waits
To pounce on Careless Children
Who stray Beyond the Gates.

Through the Forest of Fear
The Frightening Phantom glides.
In the Dark and Gloomy Glen
The Frightening Phantom hides.

In the Heart of the Forest of Fear
The Frightening Phantom lurks.
The Frightening Phantom snatches.
The Frightening Phantom smirks.

Beware the Frightening Phantom
Which lives in the Forest of Fear.
Take heed of the Witch's warning:
DON'T GO NEAR!

Poetry Patterns

Riddles and Puzzle Poems

Wordplay Poems

Riddles and Puzzle Poems

Nonsense Poems

SECTION 2
– DIFFERENT TYPES
OF POEMS

Nonsense Poems

In the Land of the Flibbertigibbets

In the land of the Flibbertigibbets,
The Curlybirds whirl and whiz,
The Googlies giggle, the Rampoons wriggle
And the Furzles flitter and fizz,
    The Furzles flitter and fizz.

In the land of the Flibbertigibbets,
The Humdrums simper and sing,
The Bamboozles bump, the Jamborees jump
And the Plimpets zip and ping,
    The Plimpets zip and ping.

In the land of the Flibbertigibbets,
The Dobblers dibble and dive,
The Clutters clatter, the Chitters chatter,
And the Junkets jiggle and jive,
    The Junkets jiggle and jive.

If You Whistle at a Thistle

If you whistle at a thistle
It'll turn its head.
If you compliment a carrot
It'll blush bright red.

If you squeeze a pickled onion
It'll start to cry.
If you cuddle a fresh cabbage
It'll softly sigh.

If you tickle a dill pickle
It'll give a girlish giggle.
If you stroke an artichoke
It'll squirm and wriggle.

If you caress a bunch of cress
It'll go quite weak.
But if you try to kiss a turnip
It'll slap you on the cheek.

On the Clip Clop Clap

(after Milligan)

On the Clip Clop Clap
All the Flops flip flap
And the Bongles boogle in the breeze.
The Sniggers snip snap,
The Trotters trip trap,
And the Somersaults sniff and sneeze
   The Somersaults sniff and sneeze.

On the Clip Clop Clap
You can never take a nap
For there's gnashing and there's thrashing in the trees
As the Bongles flex their knees.
The Flops flip flap,
The Sniggers snip snap,
The Trotters trip trap
And the Somersaults sniff and sneeze
   The Somersaults sniff and sneeze.

My Auntie Dot

My Auntie Dot's a coffee pot.
She sits on the kitchen shelf,
Waiting for someone to take her down,
Muttering to herself.

'To be a coffee pot's my lot,'
She says. 'It's rather boring.
There's nothing to do, while I sit here,
I can't even practise pouring.

'A coffee pot is not what
I'd be if I could choose.
My sister's son has far more fun,
'Cause he's a pair of shoes!'

Par for the Course

When Auntie Fey began to neigh
And spend the day just eating hay,
My uncle said, 'It's par for the course.
Your Auntie has become a horse.
I'll have to put her in the stable,
In the stall next to your Auntie Mabel!'

Auntie Arabella

Auntie Arabella grows
Geraniums between her toes.

Twining round her legs and knees
Are various colours of sweet peas.

Sitting stately on her tum
Is a gold chrysanthemum.

Sprouting from her bulbous nose
Is a beautiful red rose.

Lovingly my Uncle Ted
Tends her in her flower bed.

Uncle Frank

When we're all asleep in bed,
My Uncle Frank unscrews his head.
He fixes on another one
And sets off for a night of fun.

It really gave me quite a jolt,
The first time that I saw the bolt,
Which Uncle proudly showed to me
In the cellar after tea.

He says the reason for his fame
Is that we share a famous name:
Oh, I forgot to tell you mine,
Our family's name is Frankenstein.

The Curlapop

(after Milligan)

'What is a Curlapop, Dad?'
'It's a kind of a snake
Which lives in a box
And wears frilly socks
When it goes for a swim in the lake.'

'What does a Curlapop do, Dad?'
'It plays football with fleas.
It eats jellied eels
While turning cartwheels
And sings songs as it swings through the trees.'

'Have you seen a Curlapop, Dad?'
'On a day-trip to France,
In the town of Calais,
In a street café,
I once saw a Curlapop dance.'

'Are you sure there's a Curlapop, Dad?'
'Without any doubt, my son.
I swear by the moon
That goes green in June.
I'll take bets at a thousand to one.'

At the Animals' Fancy Dress Party

At the animals' fancy dress party
The prize for looking most cute
Was won by the Emperor Penguin
Who came in his birthday suit!

Castanets

Castanets make mischievous pets,
For if given half a chance,
They click and clack, and snap and clap,
And lead you a merry dance.

At King Neptune's Party

At King Neptune's party
The whales had a whale of a time.
The octopus did the eightsome reel
The sea slug slithered in slime.

The sea horse pranced. The dolphins danced.
The seals performed their tricks.
The eels wriggled. The jellyfish giggled.
The snapper took lots of pics.

The mermaids let their hair down.
The sea lion gave a roar.
The porpoise played. The swordfish swayed.
The crabs all waved a claw.

Flying fish did aerobatics.
The turtles did the twist.
Tuna played tunes. Oysters swooned.
Lobsters blushed and kissed.

At King Neptune's party
The whales had a whale of a time.
The octopus did the eightsome reel.
The sea slug slithered in slime.

Electric Fred

Electric Fred has wires in his head
And one hundred watt light bulbs for eyes,
Which means, of course, he can talk in morse
Or flash red, white and blue with surprise.

Just for a lark, he can shoot a spark
For three hundred feet out of his nose.
Wear rubber bands, if you shake his hands,
Or the current will tingle your toes.

Sometimes he chews a fifteen amp fuse,
Or recharges himself via the fire.
Just give him jolts of thousands of volts
And you'll find he's a really live wire!

Elastic Jones

Elastic Jones had rubber bones.
He could bounce up and down like a ball.
When he was six, one of his tricks
Was jumping a ten-foot wall.

As the years went by, Elastic would try
To jump higher, and higher, and higher.
He amazed people by jumping a steeple
Though he scratched his behind on the spire.

But, like many a star, he went too far,
Getting carried away with his power.
He boasted one day, 'Get out of my way,
I'm going to jump Blackpool Tower.'

He took off from near the end of the pier,
But he slipped and crashed into the top.
Amid cries and groans, Elastic Jones
Fell into the sea with a plop.

Aunty Joan

When Aunty Joan became a phone,
She sat there not saying a thing.
The doctor said, shaking his head,
'You'll just have to give her a ring.'

We had a try, but got no reply.
The tone was always engaged.
'She's just being silly,' said Uncle Billy.
Slamming down the receiver enraged.

'Alas, I fear,' said the engineer,
Who was called in to inspect her,
'I've got no choice. She's lost her voice.
I shall have to disconnect her.'

The phone gave a ring. 'You'll do no such thing,'
Said Aunty's voice on the line.
'I like being a phone. Just leave me alone
Or else I'll dial nine, nine, nine!'

Wordplay
Poems

Some Words

Some words whisper – soft and slow.
Some words shout – thunder, GO!
Some words scamper – patter, leap.
Some words plod – thick, chore, creep.
Some words laugh – jolly, lilt.
Some words scowl – grim and guilt.
Some words tickle – frisky, kiss.
Some words scratch – jab, jeer, hiss.

Says of the Week

Money-day. Pay away day.
Choose day. Whose day?
Wedding's day. Thick or thin day.
Furs day. Wrap up warm day.
Fries day. Hot dog day.
Sat-a-day. Armchair day.
Sons' day. Dads play.

Month by Month

Jan you really are cold.
Feb you're even colder.
March with a spring in your step.
April has a smile on her face.
Maybe the sun will shine, maybe it won't.
D'you know it's meant to be summer.
D'you lie getting a suntan
Or gusts of spray in your face?
Sept-embers glowing red cheeks.
Octo-burns the autumn leaves.
N-N-November's chillness.
Dis ember is flickering...stillness.

Doctors

Dr Aft is rough and ready.
Dr Unk's a bit unsteady.

Dr Omedary's got the hump.
Dr Ift's a snowy bump.

Dr Aught's a shivery chap.
Dr Owsy likes to nap.

Dr Um beats out a roll.
Dr Iver's in control.

Dr Agon's a fiery fighter.
Dr Acula's a late-night biter.

Saints

St Art is a beginner
who is learning how to draw.

St Rip is a tearaway
who dresses in football kit.

St Rum is a guitar player
who plays odd tunes.

St Rap is a hanger-on
with fingers snapping
and feet tap-tapping.

And St Ill is a patient,
lying in hospital, motionless.

Knights and Their Habits

Cir Cumference goes round and round.
Sur Vey looks closely at the ground.
Sur Plus is given to excess.
Sur Render yields under duress.
Sur Prise has something else in store.
Sur Charge will make you pay some more.
Sur Pass is greater in extent.
Cir Cus lives in a great big tent.
Sir Loin eats only first-class food.
Sur Ly is bad-tempered and rude.
Sur Face is quite superficial.
Cer Tificate makes it official.

Confidential: The Characters of Con Men

Con Tent	*A happy camper.*
Con Crete	*A hard man from a Greek island.*
Con Template	*A thinker and pattern designer.*
Con Queror	*Always emerges victorious.*
Con Sent	*Has an agreeable disposition.*
Con Noisseur	*A know-all.*
Con Fusion	*Always in a state of bewilderment.*
Con Undrum	*A puzzle addict.*
Con Siderate	*Kind and thoughtful.*
Con Ceited	*Full of his own self-importance.*
Con Flagration	*A fiery personality.*
Con Clusion	*Can be counted on to be there at the end.*

Questions

'What's the time?' I asked the watchdog.
'Time you were on your way,' he said with a growl.

'What's for tea?' I asked the chipmunk.
'Ask the friar,' he said. 'I just peel the potatoes.'

'Where are you?' I asked the werewolf.
'Here, there and everywhere,' he said with a grin.

'What's happened?' I asked the gnus.
'Switch on the TV and we'll tell you,' they said.

'What's the forecast?' I asked the weathercock.
'I'm blowed if I know,' he said.

Animal Apologies

'Sorry,' said the kangaroo.
'I shouldn't have jumped to conclusions.'

'Sorry,' said the camel.
'I can't help it. I've always got the hump.'

'Sorry,' said the dog.
'I've been barking up the wrong tree.'

'Sorry,' said the electric eel.
'I got my wires crossed.'

'Sorry,' said the donkey.
'I'm always making an ass of myself.'

'Sorry,' said the giraffe.
'I shouldn't have stuck my neck out.'

'Sorry,' said the crocodile.
'I shouldn't have snapped.'

Ten Things You Should Know About Hippopotamuses

1. What is a young female hippopotamus called?
   A hippopotamiss.

2. What do parents say to a young hippo when telling him not to do something?
   A hippopotamustn't.

3. How do you train a baby hippopotamus?
   By sitting him on a hippo-potty.

4. What does a hippo like spread on his burgers?
   Lots of hippopotamustard.

5. What kind of dance music does a hippopotamus like?
   Hip-hop.

6. What do you call a hippopotamus who says things behind other hippopotamuses' backs?
   A hippo-crit.

7. What do you call a hippopotamus with chicken pox?
   A hippospotamus.

8. What do you call a hippopotamus with a limp?
   A hoppopotamus.

9. What do hippopotamuses shout when they're cheering somebody?
   Hip! Hip! Hooray!

10. What do you call a hippopotamus with a smile on its face?
    A happypotamus.

Messages from Dee

Sorry. Got held up. Will be an hour late.
  D. Lay

There are two sides to everything. We must talk.
  D. Bate

You're driving me out of my mind.
  D. Mented

I'll be down in a minute.
  D. Scend.

I feel like giving up.
  D. Spair

In no way was I responsible.
  D. Ny

You can count on me.
  D. Pendable

That's it. My mind's made up.
  D. Cide

I can make your mouth water.
  D. Licious

The Word Wizard (1)

The Word Wizard said,
'Think of a word.'
What a lot of nonsense!
I thought:
Drivel.
'To find what urges you to act,'
said the Wizard,
'Subtract the last letter.'
Drive.
'Now, remove the second letter.
Go on. Take the plunge!'
Dive.
'To reveal a contraction,
Cross out the first letter.'
I've.
'Take away the middle letter
And you'll see *that* is an abbreviation.'
i.e.
'Finally, lose the last letter
And find yourself.'
I.

The Word Wizard (2)

The Word Wizard said,
Take your surname.
It's something to cherish.
Foster.
Remove the initial letter. Rotate the rest
And find a place to keep your things.
Store.
Tear away the first letter. Go on!
Now look at what you've just done!
Tore.
Carefully pick out the 'r'. But watch your step.
You don't want to tread on one of them!
Toe.
Keep going. Knock off the final letter
And point yourself in the direction you've chosen.
To.
Well done! You're getting the hang of these puzzles.
In fact, if you remove the vowel
You've got this one down to a
T.

Wordspinning

Spin pins into nips.
Snap pans into naps.
Mix spit into tips.
Turn parts into traps.

Switch post into stop.
Whisk dear into dare.
Carve hops into shop.
Rip rate into tear.

Twist tame into mate.
Make mean into name.
Juggle taste into state
In the wordspinning game.

The Name of the Game

Play with names
And Pat becomes tap.
Karl is a lark
And Pam is a map.

Miles is slime.
Liam is mail.
Bart is a brat
And Lina's a nail.

Stan tans.
Gary turns gray.
Norma's a Roman.
Amy makes May.

Tabitha's habitat.
Leon is lone.
Kate is teak.
Mona's a moan.

Trish is a shirt.
Kay is a yak.
But whatever you do
Jack remains Jack.

By Comparison

Claire's debonnaire, but Amanda is grander.
Daisy is lazy, but Jean's very keen.
Heidi's untidy, but Margarite's neat.
Bertie is dirty, but Nadine is clean.

Frankie is swanky, but Shaun is withdrawn.
Solly is jolly, but Brad's very sad.
Hannah's got manners, but Ruth is uncouth.
Pattie is batty and Maddie's quite mad.

Connie is bonny, but Jane's very plain.
Ted is well-bred, but Jude's very crude.
Lester's a jester, but Dave's very grave.
Billy's just silly, but Gertrude is rude.

Batty Booklist

Highway Robbery by Stan Dan Deliver
Cheap Ornaments by Nick Nacks
Fortune Telling by Crystal Ball
Bad Hair Days by Dan Druff
Ups and Downs by C. Saw and Ellie Vator
Keep Fit by Jim Nastics
Mouthwatering Foods by Sally Vate
Traffic Dodging by J. Walker
Make It Snappy! by Allie Gator
The Ass's Tale by Don Key
Winner Takes All by Jack Pot
Utter Nonsense by Tommy Rot

Introductions 1: Del

Hello, I'm called Del and these are my friends.
They're all called Del too!

This one's always pleased to meet you.
He'll bring a smile to your face:
Del –ight.

But take care with the second one.
He's frail and fragile:
Del –icate

The third one's a bit of a lad.
Always getting into scrapes:
Del –inquent.

The next one's a bit excitable.
He's apt to see things that aren't there:
Del –irious.

As for me, haven't you guessed?
I'm the pick of the bunch.
Sweet-smelling and mouthwatering:
Del –icious.

Introductions 2: Phil

Hello, I'm called Phil and these are my friends.
They're all called Phil too!

This one's very fond of music.
He plays in the orchestra and sings in the choir.
He's Phil –harmonic.

This one's obsessed with his hobby.
He's into stamp collecting.
He's Phil –ately.

This one works for a charity.
He's kind and benevolent.
He's Phil –anthropic.

This is the scholarly one.
He works in a university analyzing texts.
He's Phil –ologist.

Finally, there's me, wise and thoughtful.
I keep calm, taking things as they come:
I'm Phil –osophical.

Word Building (1)

The Word Wizard said:
Start at the very beginning:
A.
Be polite. Place a t in front.
Say thank you!
Ta!
Now for a cuppa!
Drop in an e.
Tea.
To find a friend,
Add in an m and stir.
Mate.
Put an s on one end.
Go on, you choose.
Either lots of friends –
Mates
Or what you need to let off
When you feel you're going to burst –
Steam.
Now insert an r
And get carried away by the flow:
Stream.
Give the letters a good shake
And you'll find out who's in charge:
Master.

Word Building (2)

The Word Wizard said:
Start with nothing:
O.
Add an r if you want an alternative:
Or.
Put a t in front
For a small hill:
Tor.
Then an e behind
To learn things parrot-fashion:
Rote.
Stir in an s
For a place to shop:
Store.
With a y on the end
It'll sound like a tale
But be one of several floors:
Storey.
Put in a d,
Shuffle the pack carefully
And you'll find a verb
That could bring the whole house down:
Destroy.

Riddle
and
Puzzle
Poems

A Ragman's Puzzle

Why is a foal like a loaf?
Why is an atom like a moat?
Why is a grin like a ring?
Why is toast like a stoat?

Why is a plum like a lump?
Why is a pager like a grape?
Why is a shrub like a brush?
Why is peat like a tape?

Why are gates like a stage?
Why is a leap like a plea?
Why is a café like a face?
Why is a leaf like a flea?

A Mixed Fruit Pie

Go man make a mango.
Add a peach that's cheap.
Pick a tangerine from the Argentine
And a pear is what you reap.

For an orange get your gear on.
For a cherry hear her cry.
Swap a lemon for a melon
And you've got a mixed fruit pie.

Riddle Me Hot, Riddle Me Cold

My first is in fish, but not in bone.
My second is in iron, but not in stone.
My third's in crown and also in throne.
My fourth's once in twice,
But twice in returned.
Touch me, get burned!

My first is in wish, but not in bone.
My second is in rock, but not in stone.
My third's once in twice,
But twice in tease.
Touch me and freeze!

Where Are We?

We are hiding everywhere.
We're wrapped up in towels.
We aren't found in consonants
But we are there in vowels!

We're there in every weather.
We're hidden in your sweater.
We're not found in water
Although we're found in wetter.

Though you'll find us in bus
We really are not there,
While only he's in here,
We're without her in where!

Find Me Out

I'm there in shout but not in scream.
I'm heard in drought but not in dream.
I am in youth but not in truth.
I'm not in booth but in uncouth.
I am in route but not in road.
I'm in about but not abode.
I'm not in north but am in south
I'm not in teeth though I'm in mouth.
I'm not in inside or inset.
I wonder have you found me yet.

Where Is It?

You'll find me in sitting, though not in sat.
I'm there in kittens, though not in cat.
I'm knotted in knitting, but not in a knot.
I'm spotted in spitting, though not in a spot.

I am in italics, but not in bold.
I am in bitter, but never in cold.
I'm in addition, but not in subtract.
I'm never in fiction, nor found in fact.

I am in itchy, but never in scratch.
I'm found in ignite, though not in a match.
I am in transit, but not in a train.
In nitwit I'm there not once but again.

I am reversed in tiptoe, but not in stride.
I go backwards in time and also in tide
When I am touched, I will join in your game.
I'm a two-letter word. That's it. That's my name!

Riddle-Me-Scared

My first is in ghoul and also in charm.
My second is in magic and twice in alarm.
My third is in cauldron but isn't in fire.
My fourth is in gremlin but not in vampire.
My fifth is in skeleton and in bones.
My sixth is in werewolf but isn't in groans.
My seventh is in spell but not in broomstick.
My eighth's found in treat, but not found in trick.
My ninth is in phantom but isn't in fear.
My whole is the scariest night of the year.

A Fortunate Find

The first of you comes last of all
And the last of all is first.
The last of you is second too
And the third of second is third.
The first of key is second to last
And so is the last of unlock.

Solve this puzzle and you'll see
How fortunate a word can be.

Staircase Poem

This is a staircase poem.
Can you find your way down,
Making very, very
Sure that you see the letter,
Especially placed on each step,
Indicating that you must
Not hurry, but
Take special *care.*

I Am Fighting This Poem

I am fighting this poem
Knitting at a cable,
Cruising a hen
And a niece of taper.
The birds are all in a huddle,
So I mope you can
Shirk out its leaning.

Football Club Anagrams

Al earns
Ava's Not Ill!
Bye Dry Count!
Dire Alien Cults
Don Wins Nowt!
Gals Anger Grows
Hum, Alf
Ill over op
Lad ends run
Man Shot Other Putt
Nice Hen Made Trust
Nothing from a test
Real new car axed
Spot hot rum
Veer Not!
Vole Trap
War! Witches Bomb Lion!
We unlace dentist
Whip cost win

Answers to riddles and Football Club Anagrams can be found on p.322

Punctuation and Spelling Poems

whatspunctuation

whatspunctuationweallneed
itsothatwecanread
whatotherswritewithoutitwed
besoconfusedwewouldnotknow
ifweshouldstoporgo
onreadingwewouldlosetheflow
ofwhatthewritermeanttosay
yeswedallloseourway
sopunctuationsheretostay

I Am a Full Stop

I am a full stop.
At my command,
sentences halt.
At its peril,
a letter which follows me
forgets it should be a capital.
I place myself between words.
I create meaning.
When children ignore me,
I cause confusion.
I am a full stop.
Learn to control *me*
and the whole written world
is yours.

I Am a Question Mark

I am a question mark.
I sit on the keyboard
Waiting to be of service
In investigations and interrogations.
I help people with their enquiries.
If you're lost,
I can help you find the way.
If you're puzzled,
I can help you search for a solution.
If there's anything you need to know
Just ask
And I'll show
That an answer's expected.

Dads Views' on Apostrophe's

Apostrophe's often appear in place's
where they are not mean't to,
like in grocery shop's windows'
advertising orange's and apple's,
or they are omitted where they shouldnt be.
Its all very confusing, isnt it?
Dad say's if hed got any say
(which he hasnt)
hed abolish the bloomin thing's.

Commas

Commas like, apostrophes
often, appear in places
where, they shouldn't,
But Dad, says
they are a different,
kettle of fish,
you need, to know
how to use, them properly,
you shouldn't just scatter them,
everywhere like, confetti,

SILENT LETTERS

We're the Silent Bs

We're the silent bs.
We can make you numb.
We can stop your chatter
By making you dumb.

We can help clean up
By picking up crumbs.
We can show we approve
By sticking up thumbs.

We can make a sheep
Give birth to a lamb.
We can hold up a door
With a wooden jamb.

We can find a plumber,
Plumb the depths of seas.
We can make you succumb.
We're the silent bs.

Silent Gees

The silent gees are coming,
They may be gnearing you.
The gnarled gnome, the gnashing gnat
And the gnasty, gnawing gnu.

The silent gees are coming.
There's gnot much you can do,
Except to feed them gnocchi
And gnotify the zoo.

Sir K

I am a silent k.
Without me
Someone might nick your knickers
Or nap in your knapsack.
You need me to be able to knead
To knock or to kneel.
I can help you
To knuckle down to knitting.
I have the knack.
Sir K, that's me –
A knowledgeable knight.

The Silent Ws

Here come the silent ws,
Writhing and wriggling along,
Wreaking havoc with your spelling –
If you write wright, that's wrong!

As you wrestle with wrinkle and wreck,
With wrapper, wrench, wretched and wrist,
Watch out for the silent ws,
They're wrathful if ever they're missed.

Spelling Mnemonic

Most	Many	Make up
Nude	Naughty	Nonsensical acrostics:
Elephants	Eels	Easily
Munch	Make	Memorise
Only	Odious	Odd
Nice	Noises	New spellings
Iced	In	In
Carrots	Cafes	Comfort

Y u lrn 2 spl

U lrn 2 spl
so u cn txt
ur frnds ezly

Life's a Spelling Test

Life's a spelling test
When I ask you, 'What's your name?'
For I may spell it differently
Although it sounds the same.

Are you Catherine with a C,
Or Katherine with a K,
Or Kathryn with a y,
Or Catharine with an a.

Is it Stephen with ph
Or Steven with a v?
Are you Glenn with double n?
Do I spell Ann(e) with an e?

Are you Sophie with ie
Or Sophy with a y?
Are you Jon without an h
Or Clare without an i?

Life's a spelling test.
It's your parents who're to blame.
What's on your birth certificate
Is how they spelt your name.

The Spelling Bee

Our teacher's got a Spelling Bee
Of which we're very wary.
It sits by itself on our teacher's shelf
Beside her dictionary.

Our teacher's got a Spelling Bee.
It buzzes round your head
Whenever you make a spelling mistake
And circles the word in red.

Our teacher's got a Spelling Bee.
We treat it with respect.
It brushes your neck as it makes a check
That your spelling is correct.

Our teacher's got a Spelling Bee.
It keeps us on our toes.
Whenever we make a spelling mistake,
The Spelling Bee always knows.

Our teacher's got a Spelling Bee
Of which we're very wary.
It sits by itself on our teacher's shelf
Beside her dictionary.

Poetry
Patterns

ACROSTICS
A Cross Stick?

A cross stick?
Can't understand what sir's
Rabbiting
On about
So I
Thought
I'd
Compose a poem instead.

Raging Toothache

Throwing a tantrum
Offensive language
Oaths and blasphemies
Terrible temper
Hollering and yelling.

Tall Story

Today, our teacher
Asked us to write
Lacrosse sticks in our English
Lesson. At least that's what we thought

She said.
That's why most
Of us looked blank and
Replied, 'If it's all right with
You, we'd rather write high queues instead.'

CINQUAINS

Blackbird

Blackbird
Hops, stops, hops, stops,
Across the lawn. Listens,
Its head cocked for sounds of a worm,
Then strikes.

At the Gate

Thoughtful,
The old man stands,
Resting against the gate,
Wondering when it will open,
Waiting.

The Wood in Late Autumn

Fog crawls
Over the wood,
Wrapping its grey blanket
Round the shivering bare shoulders
Of trees.

Mirror

Mirror
You only show
My face. But underneath
This calm exterior, my heart
Beats fast.

How to Write Cinquains?

I am
counting out the
syllables in each line
to make sure that I've written a
cinquain.

I am
not really sure
that counting syllables
is the best way to make you write
good poems.

CLERIHEWS

Neil Armstrong

Neil Armstrong
Wasn't on the moon for long.
But in that time he left behind
A giant footprint for mankind.

Count Dracula

Count Dracula
At blood-sports is quite spectacular.
He hunts for prey at dead of night
And always gets in the first bite.

John Logie Baird

John Logie Baird
Would have despaired
If he'd been able to foresee
The kind of programmes they show on TV.

EPITAPHS
Sandra Slater

Here lies what's left of Sandra Slater
Who poked her pet – an alligator –
Forgetting that to tease or bait her
Might annoy an alligator.

Alas, the alligator ate her.

Percy Thistle

Here lies the body
Of Percy Thistle,
A ref who's blown
His final whistle.

Dead End

In memory of Charlotte Cul-de-sac,
A loyal and trusted friend.
She finally lived up to her name
And came to a dead end.

In Memoriam

Here lies the body
Of Reginald Hacking.

It was his cough
That bore him off.

In Memory of Miss Chit-Chat

Beneath this stone Miss Chit-Chat lies,
Her gossiping days are done,
Her last words were as she passed away:
'I'm dying to tell someone.'

Epitaph for a Police Officer

Here lies the body
Of Constable Chest.
His heart made him
His last arrest.

Zebedee Zero

In memory of Zebedee Zero
Who dreamed of being a superhero.
Alas he failed at every sport.
His efforts always came to nought.

HAIKU

Seaview Haiku

Bright as butterflies
With folded wings, the windsurfs
Skim across the bay.

Grey as steel, the sea
Shimmers in the fading light:
Day slides into night.

A Windy Day Haiku

Anxiously, the dog
Paces the room, sniffs the door:
Outside the wind howls.

Haiku: a Book

Pages of a book
Lie in wait for eager eyes
To unfold secrets.

Haiku proverb

Wearing a gold crown
Does not turn a foolish man
Into a wise one.

KENNINGS
Volcano

Earth-rumbler
Mountain-shaker
Rock-splitter
Fissure-breaker.

Crater-cracker
Fiery fountain
Steam-spitter
Molten mountain.

Fire-breather
Lava-thrower
Moonscape-sculptor
Destruction-sower.

Alarm Clock

peace-breaker
silence-shatterer
sleep-banisher
ear-batterer

day-herald
bell-ringer
dream-ending
morning-bringer

LIMERICKS

There Once Was a Boy Called Bill

There once was a boy called Bill
Who sat on a porcupine's quill.
He jumped in the air
'Cause his bottom was bare
And that's why he cannot sit still.

There Once Was a Boy Called Jack

There once was a boy called Jack
Who went for a ride on a yak.
When he gave it a smack
It raced off down the track
And came back without Jack on its back.

SHAPE POEMS
Concrete Poems

<pre>
       concrete poems
       are hard to read
          pneumatic
            drills
             are
            what
             Y
             O
             U
             N
             E
             E
             D
  concrete poems are hard to crack
 it's builders who have got the knack
</pre>

A Traffic Queue

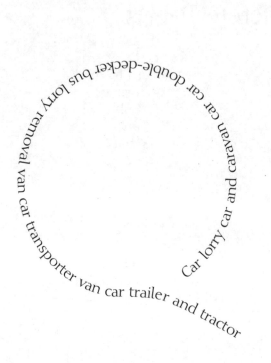

Car lorry car and caravan car car double-decker bus lorry removal van car transporter van car trailer and tractor

Staple Diet

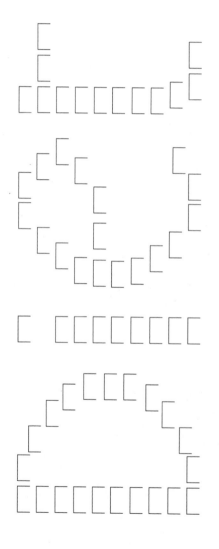

Child Skipping

```
            ki
      s          p
            ki
      s          p
            ki
      s          p
            ki
      s          p
            ki
      s          p
            ki
      s          p
            ki
      s          p .
            ki
      s          p
            ki
      s          p
            ki
```

Ball Bouncing

Factory

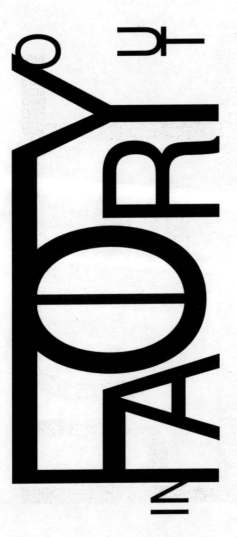

Hotel

Belt

I am a belt. Thread me carefully around your waist and fasten me tight or I might let you down.

Diamond Poem

Spark
Glows red
In wind's breath.
Struggles for   life.
Flickers. Dies. Flickers.
Bursts into flame.
Twists and leaps.
Dancing
Fire.

Numbers

1   is a tall man all alone;
    a sentry standing to attention.
2   is a coatpeg with a tail.
3   is a torn leaf, fluttering on the page.
4   is a kite which has lost its string.
5   is an iron fish-hook.
6   is an earpiece left behind by a walkman.
7   is a broken arrow.
8   is an acrobat – one ball balancing on another.
9   is a ladle for serving soup.
10 is a knife lying beside an empty plate.

Word Whirls

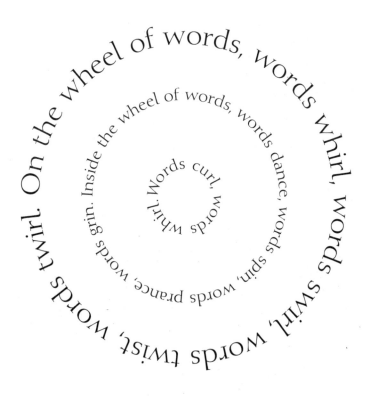

On the wheel of words, words whirl, words swirl, words twist, words twirl. Inside the wheel of words, words dance, words prance, words spin, words whirl. Words curl, words whirl.

Thin Poems

Thin poems slide down the window pane

of the page like tears, slip under

doors leaving messages of farewell

then disappear like whispers in the wind

I

I M P R E S S I V E
I N D I V I D U A L
I N D E P E N D E N T

```
              I
    I         S         I
    N         O         N
    S         L         S
    U         A         U
    L         T         L
    A         E         A
    R         D         R
```

ISLAND I ISLAND

I M P E R I O U S

TANKA
Silver Aeroplane

Silver aeroplane
Speeds across the summer sky
Leaving in its wake
Trails of vapour: White scribblings
On a page of blue paper.

The Penny Black

This is my best stamp
And it's the most valuable
Because my Grandad
Gave it to me last summer
On the day before he died.

TONGUE-TWISTERS
Shaun Short's Short Shorts

Shaun Short bought some shorts.
The shorts were shorter than Shaun Short thought.
Shaun Short's short shorts were so short,
Shaun Short thought, Shaun, you ought
Not to have bought shorts so short.

Nicola Nicholas

Nicola Nicholas couldn't care less.
Nicola Nicholas tore her dress.
Nicola Nicholas tore her knickers.
Now Nicola Nicholas is knickerless.

Boris Morris's Sister Doris

Boris Morris had a sister Doris.
Horace Norris had a brother Maurice.
Boris Morris's sister Doris
Married Horace Norris's brother Maurice.
So Doris Morris became Doris Morris-Norris.

Quite Right, Mrs Wright

On the night before the first night of *Twelfth Night*
Dwight Wright had stagefright
And Mrs Wright said, 'Don't get uptight, Dwight,
It'll be all right on the night.'

On the night after the first night of *Twelfth Night*
Dwight Wright said, 'In spite
Of being uptight with stagefright, it went all right.
You were quite right, Mrs Wright.'

Who'll Go, If You'll Go

Do you know Hugo?
He'll go if I'll go
And Hugh'll go, if you'll go.
So...Hugo'll go and Hugh'll go
If I go and you go.
That's who'll go, if you'll go.

Sue Shore Shrieked

Sue Shore shrieked.
Sue Shore shouted, 'Shoo!'
Sue was sure she saw
A shrew in her shoe.

Underwood's Underwear

Underwood would wear underwear
If Underwood knew where
Underwood put
Underwood's underwear.

Did Underwood put his underwear
Under here or over there?
Did Underwood put his underwear
Under or over the chair?

I wonder, wonder where
Underwood put
Underwood's underwear?

Six Sick Sikhs Met Six Sick Sheiks

Six sick Sikhs met six sick sheiks.
'Shake hands,' said the Sikhs.
'Shake hands,' said the sheiks.
'We're sick of being sick,'
said the six sick Sikhs.
'We're sick of being sick,'
said the six sick sheiks.
Six Sikhs with the shivers.
Six sheikhs with the shakes.

STORY POEMS
When Allie Had a Loose Tooth

When Allie had a loose tooth,
She did as her dad said.
She went into the kitchen
And found a piece of thread.

She tied it round the tooth.
She tied it to the door.
But when she slammed the door shut,
The knob fell on the floor!

Not a Good Day

Diary entry for Saturday, 24th June

Got up at half-past nine.
Match day. Felt fine.

Kit packed. No fuss.
Twelve o'clock. Caught bus.

One o'clock. At ground.
First there. Wandered round.

Two o'clock. Toss won.
Batting first. Pads on.

Oh no! Just my luck.
Played on. A golden duck.

Three thirty. Early tea.
All out for 53.

Four o'clock. Bowled no ball.
Hit for six over wall.

Five o'clock. Dropped catch.
Five thirty. Lost match.

Dad's Hiding in the Shed

Dad's hiding in the shed.
He's made me swear
Not to tell Mum
That he's hiding in there.

She was having a lie-down
With the curtains drawn.
We were playing cricket
Out on the lawn.

The scores were level.
It was really tense.
Dad had just hit a six
Right over the fence.

I bowled the next ball
As fast as I could.
Dad tried it again
As I knew he would.

He missed and the ball
Struck him hard on the toe.
He cried out in pain
And, as he did so,

He let go of the bat.
It flew up in an arc
And crashed through the window
Where Mum lay in the dark.

Dad's hiding in the shed.
He's made me swear
Not to tell Mum
That he's hiding in there.

Show Me Your Scar, Please, Grandad

'Show me your scar, please, Grandad.
Show me the scar on your knee.
Tell me the story, please, Grandad
Of how you fell out of the tree.'

Grandad rolled up his trousers
To show me the wrinkled skin
And pointed out where the doctor
Had put all the stitches in.

'We were having a game of football
One afternoon after tea,
When your Great-Uncle Bill miskicked
And the ball got stuck up the tree.

We tried throwing sticks to knock it out
But we didn't have any luck.
Most of them missed and the others bounced off
'Cause the ball was firmly stuck.

So we fetched the ladder from the shed
And propped it against the tree,
And I climbed to the top and caught hold
Of a branch to try to shake the ball free.

I leaned over too far and my foot slipped.
The branch broke with a crack.
I fell through the tree and the next thing I knew
I was lying on the ground on my back.

I looked down at my leg. There was blood everywhere
And a terrible pain in my knee.
Bill took one look, then ran off to fetch help,
Shouting, 'Jack's fallen out of the tree!'

An ambulance came and they took me away,
Put in stitches and bandaged my knee,
And that's how I came to get this scar
The day I fell out of the tree.

Everything's Fine

First, we missed the turning on the motorway.
Don't ask me how!
I'd fallen asleep in the back.
I was woken by the shouting
As they tried to blame each other.
We had to drive another twelve miles
To the next junction
And another twelve miles back.
By that time it was dark.
It took us another half-hour
To find the campsite.
It's down this narrow lane.
Half-way along we met another car.
The driver just sat there.
So we had to reverse
All the way back to the main road.
By the time we got to reception,
It was closed.
It took us twenty minutes
To find the warden.
He kept complaining
That he was off duty.
Then, he couldn't find our booking-form.
'We're full up,' he said,
'Apart from the overflow field
And we're not really supposed to use that
At this time of year.'
You can tell why it's called
The overflow field.
The mud's inches thick

And it's right next to the toilet block.
I've left them putting the tent up.
I'm just phoning to let you know
We've arrived safely
And everything's fine.

The Mermaid and the Fisherman

By a cave of coral the mermaid sits
Beneath a silvery moon
And the lonely fisherman hears her voice
As she sings a haunting tune.

He forgets his nets and he grabs the oars
And he swings the boat around
To head for the shore for he must hear more
Of the soft bewitching sound.

By a cave of coral the mermaid smiles
Hearing the splash of an oar
And the grating of pebbles on the beach
As a boat is pulled ashore.

The fisherman stands in front of the cave
With a wild look in his eyes.
On a seaweed bed in a coral cave
An enchanting mermaid lies.

The fisherman reaches out with his hand
To touch her silvery hair
And the mermaid smiles as she lures him down
To capture him in her lair.

In a coral cave a fisherman sits,
Spellbound at a mermaid's side.
On the beach above an abandoned boat
Is lapped by the morning tide.

The Man With a Map

Sitting in a bar
In many a seaside town
You'll see a man with a faraway look,
His face creased into a frown.

He looks a scruffy sort.
His shirt is tattered and torn.
His hair is greasy and matted.
His boots are scuffed and worn.

Tattooed on his forearm,
There's a skull and crossbones flag
And on the floor, beside his chair,
There's an ancient canvas bag.

In front of him on the table,
A parchment map is spread.
As he scrutinises it closely,
He slowly shakes his head.

He's searching for the spot
Where they dug a hole and hid
The chests that held the treasure
Plundered by Captain Kidd.

But the ink on the map has faded.
The paper is cracked and dry.
As he looks in vain for a cross,
He heaves a heavy sigh.

You can see him in a bar
In many a seaside town,
A pirate with a faraway look,
His face creased into a frown.

The Smugglers

Through the sea-mist
Two small boats glide,
Slipping ashore
On the evening tide.

A man with a lantern
Flashes a light
To warn those on shore,
'We're coming tonight.'

A messenger hurries
From door to door,
Whispering softly,
'They're coming ashore.'

Down the cliff path
Six shadows glide
To the foot of the cliff
Where they crouch and hide.

They watch and wait,
Not saying a word,
Until the sound
Of the oars is heard.

Then, quickly, they hurry
Across the sand.
The barrels are passed
From hand to hand.

They are stacked in the cave
And hidden away
Till it's safe to move them
Another day.

Then, back to their beds
The shadows glide,
While the boats slip away
On the outgoing tide.

Writing Poems of Your Own

Why not have a try at writing some poems of your own? Here are ways of using some of the poems in this book to get you started.

SECTION 1 – THEMES

Family Poems

■ Think about times when you've done something at home and you've been waiting for your parents to find out, as the children are doing in 'The Vase' (p32.). Use your experience as the starting point for either a free verse or a rhyming poem.

■ Read 'Parents!' (p.40). Make a list of all the things that grown-ups do which you find embarrassing. Draft a similar free verse poem 'Grown-Ups! They're so embarrassing!'

■ Remind yourself what a metaphor is (p.305). Then read 'Grandma Is a Warm Scarf' (p.43) Pattern a similar poem about another member of your family, in which you compare them to different things, such as a piece of clothing, a food or drink etc.

Feelings Poems

■ Use a happy memory or a sad memory as the starting point for a free verse poem expressing your feelings about what happened. You could start it 'I remember the time...'

■ Remind yourself what a cinquain is (p.302) and what a metaphor is (p.305), then read 'Anger' (p.54) Use it as a model for a poem about another feeling, such as joy, fear, envy, hatred or hope.

School Poems

■ With some friends, draft an extra verse to add to 'Children's Prayer' (p.65), then work out a performance of the poem, which includes your extra verse.

■ Study 'The Schoolkids' Rap' (p.82) and then write your own rap. You could write it about your school e.g. The St John's School Rap or about any topic you choose. You could use these two lines to start it:

Come on everybody, let's hear you clap,
We're going to do the...... rap.

Football Poems

■ Write your own poem about football. You could write a poem in the form of a diary entry about a particular game in which you played or an incident that occurred when you were having a kickabout, or you could write from a fan's point of view about what it's like being a fan. Alternatively, you could write your own football dream poem similar to 'The Night I Won the Cup' (p.86)

- Read 'Nonsense Football Rhymes' (p.95). Think of some other nursery rhymes and write some nonsense football versions of your own.

Bullying Poems

- Read all the poems in this section, then write a poem which expresses your thoughts about bullying and what it feels like if you're the person being bullied. You could start your poem with a question such as ' Why do you pick on me?' or 'How would you feel?' It could be either a free verse or a rhyming poem.

War Poems

- Think about the viewpoints of war that are expressed in the poems in this section. Then think about the images of war that you have seen on TV news bulletins and documentaries. You could use one or more of these images as the starting point for your own poem about war and its effects.

Poems About Our World

- What concerns you about the environment? Write your own protest poem about the way human behaviour is affecting the environment. You could model your poem on one of the poems in this section or develop your poem in the form that best helps you to express your ideas.

Weather Poems

■ Read 'The Wild Wind' (p.138) and 'When the Wind Blows' (p.138). Think about what it is like to be out on a very windy day. Draft a list poem 'On a Windy Day'. Try to include some similes e.g. 'Leaves scuttle across the road like frightened mice.'

■ Use 'What is Fog?'(p.142) as a model and write a similar poem in which you make comparisons e.g. 'What is Snow?'.

Seasons Poems

■ Remind yourself what a haiku is (p.303) Read 'Spring Haiku' (p.150), then draft your own haiku in which you create a picture which encapsulates another of the seasons: summer haiku, autumn haiku or winter haiku.

■ Write a poem 'Recipe for a Winter's Day' in the form of a recipe, similar to 'Recipe for a Summer Holiday' (p.152). First make a list of all the ingredients for a winter's day, then draft them into the pattern of a recipe.

■ Remind yourself what a metaphor is (p.305) Use 'November' (p.155) as a model for a poem about another month e.g. 'February is a frozen pond...'

Animals Poems

■ Read 'It's a Dog's Life' (p.160) and 'Mrs Nugent's Budgie' (p.163). Think about times when there have been incidents involving either one of your pets or a neighbour's pet. Perhaps next door's rabbit escaped or your dog ate the joint of meat you were going to have for dinner. Write a free verse poem about the incident.

■ Read 'Bird Talk' (p.166). Notice how what each bird says tells you something about its character. Draft some similar poems in the form of statements from other birds e.g. Swoop the hawk, Scavenger the crow or statements from animals e.g. Slowcoach the snail, Snapper the crocodile.

Dinosaur and Dragon Poems

■ Remind yourself what a couplet is (p.303) Read 'Ten Dancing Dinosaurs' (p.176) then write your own poem in rhyming couplets about monsters (Ten Mighty Monsters) or dragons (Ten Naughty Dragons).

■ Make a list of questions that you would ask a dinosaur if you had the chance to interview it. Then read 'Interview with a Dragon' (p.180) and draft a similar poem 'Interview with a Dinosaur'.

Wizard, Ghost and Vampire Poems

■ Read 'Love Letter – From the Wizard to the Witch' (p.190) Then draft a reply from the witch in which she tells the wizard that she finds him attractive too. You could start 'I love your blackened fingernails./ I love your greasy hair…'

■ Write a riddle poem similar to 'Riddle Me a Count' (p.194) in which the reader has to find a word such as skeleton, coffin, werewolf or ghoul.

SECTION 2 – DIFFERENT TYPES OF POEMS

Nonsense Poems

■ Read 'My Auntie Dot' (p.205), 'Par for the Course'(p.205) and 'Aunty Joan' (p.212), then draft your own nonsense poem about a relative who turns into an object e.g. 'My Uncle Mike's a motorbike…' or 'When Uncle Brian became a lion…'

■ Read 'In the Land of the Flibbertigibbets'(p.202) Make up a poem about a nonsense land in which everything is different. For example, you could develop a poem in couplets about the land of Hullabaloo beginning: 'In the Land of Hullabaloo/ The grass is a brilliant blue…'

Wordplay Poems

■ 'Word Wizard (1)' (p.223) and 'Word Wizard (2)' (p.224) are poems that develop by taking apart a word letter by letter, each time finding another word. See if you can develop a similar poem either by finding a word that you can take apart in this way or by starting with one of these words – tablets, glisten. 'Word Building (1)' (p.231) and 'Word Building (2)' (p.232) work in the opposite direction, building up words letter by letter. Start with any letter of the alphabet and try to build up to a word consisting of six or seven letters.

■ 'Introductions 1: Del' (p.229) and 'Introductions 2: Phil' (p.230) both play with words that start with a syllable which forms a person's first name. Use the poems as models and draft your own poems that begin with a syllable which is a person's name e.g. Ann, Ben

Riddles and Puzzle Poems

■ Remind yourself what an anagram is (p.301) Read 'A Ragman's Puzzle' (p.234) and draft one or two verses to add to the poem.

■ Read 'Where Are We?' (p.235), 'Find Me Out' (p.236) and 'Where Is It?' (p.236) Draft a similar rhyming poem which consists of words which have an 'in' hidden in them e.g. contain, destination, mine.

Punctuation and Spelling Poems

■ Read 'I am a Full Stop' (p.242) and 'I am a Question Mark' (p.243). Draft a similar poem in which another punctuation mark states what it does.

Poetry Patterns

■ Remind yourself what an acrostic is (p.301) and read the three acrostics (p.252/3). Then write your own acrostic. You can write an acrostic about anything from a tractor to treasure, from a spider to your name.

■ Remind yourself what a clerihew is (p.302) and study the three clerihews (p.256) Write some clerihews about characters from nursery rhymes and traditional tales e.g. Cinderella, Little Bo Peep, Little Jack Horner.

- Read the cinquains (p.254/5) and 'How To Write Cinquains?' (p.255) Remind yourself what a cinquain is (p.302), then try to write a cinquain on a subject of your own. In addition to making sure that your poem has the right number of syllables per line, make sure that the poem expresses a thought or feeling about the subject.

- Read the epitaphs (p.257-9), then draft some epitaphs of your own. Here are some people you could write epitaphs for – a teacher called Mr Head, a weather forecaster called Gail, an inventor called Mr Sprocket; or you could write an epitaph for an alien, a dinosaur or a troll.

- Read 'Seaview Haiku' (p.260) Remind yourself what a haiku is (p.303) and write one or two haiku of your own describing scenes e.g. fairground haiku, lakeside haiku or woodland haiku.

- Remind yourself what a kenning is (p.304) Read the kennings poems on page 261, then draft a kennings poem of your own. You could choose your own subject or write about one of these subjects: wind, sea, fire, horse, mobile phone.

- Read the two limericks (p.262). Remind yourself of the pattern of a limerick (p.304) and try to write a limerick of your own. Here are some first lines you could use: 'A wizard's apprentice called Jake…', 'There was a young girl called Jane…', 'There was a young man called Paul…'

- 'Belt' (p.270) is a common type of shape poem in which the words form the shape of the object that is being described. Write a similar shape poem of your own e.g. about a shoe, a knife, a pencil or any object that you choose.

■ Use 'Numbers' (p.272) as a model and draft your own poem about the shape of the numbers from 1-10. Think carefully about what each of the shapes is like and be prepared to have to take time. Some numbers are harder to do than others!

■ Study the concrete poem about the letter 'I' (p.275). Ask yourself why each of the words has been chosen and what message about I each particular word gives. Then draft your own concrete poem by fitting words inside the shape of another letter e.g. the letter C.

■ Remind yourself about the pattern of tanka (p.308) Read 'Silver Aeroplane' (p.276) and write a tanka of your own about another form of transport e.g. an ocean liner, a helicopter, a racing car, a motorbike.

■ Read the tongue-twisters on pages 276-279. Remind yourself what alliteration is (p.301) Make a list of words that start with the same sound e.g. ch- cr- st- tr-, then fit them together to make a tongue-twister. It doesn't matter if your tongue-twister doesn't make sense e.g. 'A chocolate chicken cheerfully chewing cheese.'

Story Poems

■ Read 'Not a Good Day' (p.281) Think about a day that you remember because it was a very good day or a very bad day. Use the memory as the starting point for a story poem of your own. You could either write it in the form of a diary poem like 'Not a Good Day' or you could write it as a free verse poem.

Glossary

- **ACROSTIC:** a poem in which certain letters of a word in each line together form a word, which is the subject of the poem.

- **ADJECTIVE:** an adjective is a word that tells you more about a noun by describing it, for example, 'heavy', 'green':
  An adjective describes a noun
  Like bright, delicious, cold or brown.

- **ADVERB:** an adverb is a word that tells you more about a verb by describing it. Many adverbs end in –ly e.g. 'brightly', 'slowly'
  An adverb describes a verb
  Like shining brightly,
  Smiling sweetly
  Or gripping tightly.

- **ALLITERATION:** the use of several words together that all begin with the same letter or sound, e.g. digs down deep.

- **ANAGRAM:** an anagram is a word or phrase consisting of letters which can be rearranged to form another word e.g. pots/stop/spot/tops.

- **ASSONANCE:** the repetition of the same vowel sound with different consonants e.g. night/time.

- **BALLAD:** a type of poem or song which tells a story. It usually consists of a number of short verses with a strong beat or rhythm to keep the story moving at a fast pace.

- **CALLIGRAM:** a poem in which either the handwriting (the calligraphy), the formation of the letters or the typeface used, represents a feature of the subject e.g. **Shivering trees freeze**.

- **CHORUS:** a section of a poem or song that is repeated after each verse has been spoken or sung.

- **CINQUAIN:** a form of syllable poem consisting of five lines adding up to 22 syllables. Line 1 has two syllables, line 2 has four syllables, line 3 has six syllables, line 4 has eight syllables and line 5 has two syllables. It was invented by the American poet Adelaide Crapsey.

- **CLERIHEW:** a four-line verse about a person, which consists of two rhyming couplets. The first line of a clerihew is the name of the person. Finding words which rhyme with people's names isn't easy, so clerihews are difficult to write. The verse takes its name from Edmund Clerihew Bentley who invented it.

- **CONCRETE POEM:** a concrete poem is a type of poem in which the layout of a word or words is designed to represent a feature of the subject.

- **COUPLET:** a couplet is a pair of consecutive lines that rhyme.

- **COUNTING RHYME:** a rhyming poem in which counting of some kind plays a significant part e.g.
  Crocodile one, alligator two
  Who's been causing a hullabaloo?
  Elephant three, rhinoceros four
  Who's been banging on the kitchen door?...

- **DIAMOND POEM:** a diamond poem is a type of poem with a certain number of syllables in each line, so that the poem forms the shape of a diamond.

- **ELEGY:** a poem or song written in memory of a person or animal that has died.

- **EPITAPH:** a short piece of writing that is put on the gravestone of a person who has died. Poets enjoy making up humorous epitaphs for unusual people.

- **FIGURATIVE LANGUAGE:** the language used in metaphors and similes to create imagery in a poem.

- **FREE VERSE:** any poem which does not have a regular pattern of rhyme or metre.

- **HAIKU:** a traditional Japanese verse-form, consisting of three lines and a total of seventeen syllables, arranged in the pattern 5-7-5.

- **HALF-RHYMES:** these are words that nearly rhyme e.g. slip/clap. If you can't think of a full rhyme that makes sense, it is usually better to use a half-rhyme than a full rhyme that makes no sense at all.

- **IMAGE:** a picture created in the mind by the words a poet uses and the ideas they suggest.

- **IMAGERY:** the way language is used in a poem to create images, through careful choice of vocabulary and the use of metaphors and similes.

- **INTERNAL RHYME:** a rhyme that is used within a line of poetry.

- **KENNING:** a kenning is a descriptive phrase, or compound word, which is used to name something instead of using a noun. Anglo-Saxon poets often used kennings in their poems, for example, a river is sometimes described as 'the swan-path'. A kennings poem is a poem consisting of a list of kennings.

- **LETTER POEM:** a poem that is written in the form of a letter.

- **LIMERICK:** a limerick is a humorous five-line poem with a particular pattern, first made popular by the nineteenth century poet Edward Lear. It has a rhyme scheme of aabba: lines 1 and 2 are longer lines of three beats ending with a rhyme; lines 3 and 4 are shorter lines of two beats that end with a rhyme; line 5 is a longer line of three beats that rhymes with lines 1 and 2. There are many anonymous limericks, for example:

There was a young girl from Gloucester
Whose parents thought they had lost her.
From the fridge came a sound
At last she was found.
The trouble was – how to defrost her?

■ **LIST POEM:** any poem in which you develop the ideas in the form of a list e.g. a list of batty books.

■ **METAPHOR:** a way of describing something or someone as though it were something else, in order to put a picture or an idea into your reader's mind through the comparison you make e.g. Grandma is a warm scarf.

■ **METRE:** the pattern of stressed and unstressed syllables in a line of poetry.

■ **MONOLOGUE:** a monologue is a long speech given by a character in a play or a film, often when the person is alone. A poem can be written in the form of a monologue as if a character is speaking their thoughts aloud.

■ **NARRATIVE POEM:** a poem which tells a story.

■ **NONSENSE POEM:** a poem which describes nonsensical people, events or things or which uses nonsense words.

- **NOUN:** a noun is any word that is the name of a thing, a person, a feeling or an idea.

  A noun is the name of anything
  like car or soap or love or ring.
  A noun is the name of a person too
  like Jason, Wasim, Jill or Lou.
  A noun is also the name of a place –
  Pakistan, Glasgow, Mars or Space.
  A noun's any kind of naming word –
  bluebottle, Bill, Bolton, bird.

- **ONOMATOPOEIA:** the use of a word or words that sound like and suggest the noise or action that is being described e.g. hiss, clatter, hum.

- **PARODY:** a poem which is written in imitation of the style of another poem e.g 'All things dry and dusty' (p.122) is a parody of 'All things bright and beautiful'.

- **PERFORMANCE POEM:** any poem written in such a way that it can be performed by an individual or group.

- **PERSONIFICATION:** the giving of human characteristics to an animal or an object and referring to it as if it were a person

- **RAP:** a rap, or rap poem, has a strong rhythmic beat and is often spoken to music. Raps are to be spoken and performed, so they contain lots of words and phrases that are common in speech.

- **RECIPE POEM:** a poem that is set out like the instructions for a recipe in a cookery book.

- **REFRAIN:** part of a poem which is repeated regularly, like the chorus of a song.

- **RHYME:** words that have the same end sounds are said to rhyme.

- **RHYME SCHEME:** the pattern of rhymes in a verse or a poem. You can describe the pattern by giving each rhyme a letter. In the example (below), the rhyme scheme is abab.

   When the night is as cold as stone,
   When lightning severs the sky,
   When your blood is chilled to the bone,
   That's the hour when the witches fly.

- **RHYTHM:** our sense of the movement or beat of a line of poetry made by the way the syllables are stressed or unstressed.

- **RIDDLE:** a riddle poem is one in which you write about something without telling the reader what it is, so the readers have to work out the meaning for themselves.

- **SHAPE POEM**: a shape poem is one in which the lines of the poem are arranged to make a picture or shape. You can make a shape poem about any kind of object. In the simplest form of shape poem, the words are written so that they make the shape of the object.

- **SIMILE:** a simile is when you compare one thing to another in order to create an image in the reader's mind, using 'like' or 'as' to make the comparison, e.g. 'the shark's teeth are like a row of daggers'; 'as cold as a witch's icy glare'.

- **SONNET:** a rhyming poem of fourteen lines with the same metrical pattern. Two typical rhyme schemes are: ababcdcdefefgg and abba abba followed by two or three other rhymes in the remaining six lines.

- **STANZA:** a verse or section of a poem, the pattern of which is repeated throughout the poem. In a printed poem, one stanza is separated from the next by a space.

- **SYLLABLE:** a unit of sound which forms a word or part of a word, e.g. 'band' has one syllable, 'bandstand' has two syllables, 'bandmaster' has three syllables. You can work out how many syllables a word has by counting the number of beats in it. A syllable poem is one which has a pattern according to the number of syllables in each line. Haiku and tanka are examples of syllable poems.

- **TANKA:** a type of Japanese syllable poem, consisting of five lines and 31 syllables arranged in the pattern 5-7-5-7-7.

- **THIN POEM:** a poem in which each line consists of only a few letters or words so that it looks thin.

- **TONGUE-TWISTER:** a rhyme that is difficult to say properly because it uses similar or repeated sounds e.g. 'She sells sea-shells on the sea shore'.

- **TRIOLET:** a French verse-form, consisting of eight lines, with the first line and the second line repeated as refrains and a rhyming pattern of abaaabab that uses only two rhymes. Lines 1, 4 and 7 are the same and lines 2 and 8 are the same.

- **VERB:** a verb is a word which tells you what people or things are doing or being.

  A verb is a special kind of word.
  It tells you of something being done,
  Like swim or talk, eat or walk,
  Creep or crawl or run.
  A verb is a word that tells you
  What people or things are doing,
  Like shining or glowing,
  Swallowing or chewing.

- **VERSE:** a patterned set of lines in a poem, which is repeated throughout the poem. A common verse-form is the four-line verse called a quatrain.

- **WORDPLAY:** a wordplay poem is any poem which plays with words and their meanings.

Index of Different Types of Poem

■ HAIKU

■ HUMOUR

■ RIDDLE

■ SHAPE

ANSWERS TO RIDDLES

Riddle Me a Count (p194): Dracula
Riddle Me Hot, Riddle Me Cold (p235): fire, ice
Riddle-Me-Scared (p237): Halloween
A Fortunate Find (p237): lucky

ANSWERS TO FOOTBALL CLUB ANAGRAMS (P240)

Al earns – Arsenal
Ava's Not Ill! – Aston Villa
Bye Dry Count! – Derby County
Dire Alien Cults! – Carlisle United
Don Wins Nowt! – Swindon Town
Gals Anger Grows – Glasgow Rangers
Hum Alf – Fulham
Ill over op – Liverpool
Lad ends run – Sunderland
Man Shot Other Putt – Tottenham Hotspur
Nice Hen Made Trust – Manchester United
Nothing from a test – Nottingham Forest
Read new car axed – Crewe Alexandra
Spot hot rum – Portsmouth
Veer Not! – Everton
Vole Trap – Port Vale
War! Witches Bomb Lion! – West Bromwich Albion
We unlace dentist – Newcastle United
Whip cost win – Ipswich Town

Index of Titles

Index of First Lines